Praise for *The Power of Having Fun*

"The simple wisdom in Dave's book migh~~t just~~ ～～～ ～～～ ～"
—**Seth Godin, author of *What to Do When It's Your Turn***

"Let's face it, the nine-to-five workday is a thing of the past. Dave really gets that the companies that will ultimately succeed are those that embrace the flexible workday and empower their employees."
—**Brian Halligan, cofounder and CEO, HubSpot**

"Don't let the apparent lightness of this fun book about having fun deceive you. There is some serious science and old-fashioned good sense in this book/workbook. It's a call to disrupt our constant action with simple activities—oases in the desert—that rest and refresh us for not just greater productivity but greater happiness and satisfaction in our work and life."
—**Whitney Johnson, author of *Disrupt Yourself***

"Dave Crenshaw's *The Power of Having Fun* is a serious book for jump-starting your life's ambitions and your career goals. 'Having fun' finally gets the attention it deserves as an important technology for successfully getting things done. So many people need this book!"
—**"Famous Dave" Anderson, America's Rib King, founder of Famous Dave's and Jimmie's Old Southern BBQ Smokehouse**

"Can you be more productive by having more fun? Dave Crenshaw's book made me a believer. His Oasis Breaks should be an essential part of your time management strategy."
—**Laura Stack, CPAE Hall of Fame Speaker and author of *Doing the Right Things Right***

"My name is Sean and I am a fun addict. If it's not fun, I'm not doing it. That's why I love this book. My buddy Dave teaches you why having fun can actually make you more productive. You need to have more fun—read this book to find out how."
—**Dr. Sean Stephenson, author of *Get Off Your "But"***

"The principles Dave teaches in this book have helped me be not only a more productive leader but a more grounded human being. Dave's influence in my life and career has been invaluable."
—**Catherine Hoke, founder and CEO, Defy Ventures**

"A masterful guide to freedom of time and creation of true joy. This book keeps its promise to make you richer—financially, yes, but also to find wealth money can't buy: time with loved ones. Dave Crenshaw helped me achieve new levels of financial success, all the while cutting my workweek in half. I've never been happier. Business has never been better."

—**Jason Hewlett, CPAE Hall of Fame Speaker**

"Crenshaw provides a powerful system for making fun a vital part of your business strategy. Highly recommended."

—**Asher Raphael, Co-CEO and Partner, Power Home Remodeling**

The
POWER
of HAVING
FUN

HOW **MEANINGFUL BREAKS**
HELP **YOU GET MORE DONE***

and Feel Fantastic!

DAVE CRENSHAW

Berrett–Koehler Publishers, Inc.
a BK Life book

Berrett-Koehler Publishers, Inc.

1333 Broadway, Suite 1000, Oakland, CA 94612-1921

Tel: (510) 817-2277 • Fax: (510) 817-2278 • www.bkconnection.com

ORDERING INFORMATION

QUANTITY SALES. Special discounts are available on quantity purchases by corporations, associations, and others. For details, contact the "Special Sales Department" at the Berrett-Koehler address above.

INDIVIDUAL SALES. Berrett-Koehler publications are available through most bookstores. They can also be ordered directly from Berrett-Koehler: Tel: (800) 929-2929; Fax: (802) 864-7626; www.bkconnection.com

ORDERS FOR COLLEGE TEXTBOOK/COURSE ADOPTION USE. Please contact Berrett-Koehler: Tel: (800) 929-2929; Fax: (802) 864-7626.

ORDERS BY U.S. TRADE BOOKSTORES AND WHOLESALERS. Please contact Ingram Publisher Services, Tel: (800) 509-4887; Fax: (800) 838-1149; E-mail: customer .service@ingrampublisherservices.com; or visit www.ingrampublisherservices.com/ Ordering for details about electronic ordering.

Berrett-Koehler and the BK logo are registered trademarks of Berrett-Koehler Publishers, Inc.

Printed in Canada

Berrett-Koehler books are printed on long-lasting acid-free paper. When it is available, we choose paper that has been manufactured by environmentally responsible processes. These may include using trees grown in sustainable forests, incorporating recycled paper, minimizing chlorine in bleaching, or recycling the energy produced at the paper mill.

LIBRARY OF CONGRESS CATALOGING-IN-PUBLICATION DATA

Names: Crenshaw, Dave, 1975- author.

Title: The power of having fun : how meaningful breaks help you get more done (and feel fantastic!) / by Dave Crenshaw.

Description: Oakland : Berrett-Koehler Publishers, 2017. | Includes index.

Identifiers: LCCN 2017019306 | ISBN 9781523083534 (pbk.)

Subjects: LCSH: Time management. | Rest periods. |
Pleasure--Psychological
aspects. | Performance. | Work.

Classification: LCC BF637.T5 C74 2017 | DDC 650.1/1--dc23

LC record available at https://lccn.loc.gov/2017019306

First Edition

22 21 20 19 18 17   10 9 8 7 6 5 4 3 2 1

Cover design: Sue Malikowski and John Arce. Interior illustrations: Abu Khalid. Book production and interior design: VJB/Scribe. Copyediting: John Pierce. Proofreading: Nancy Bell. Index: Theresa Duran.

To my wife
You're always right . . . most of the time.

CONTENTS

PART THREE: The Family Oasis

PART FOUR: The Work Oasis

APPENDIX

Introduction. Seriously.

Before we begin, I need to clear the air.

This is not a book about fun.

This is a book about *having* fun.

You may be thinking, "Oh, great. I'm not even one hundred words in, and this guy has already pulled the rug out from under me!" But hold on a second. If you stick with me, you'll understand that the point I'm making is vital.

If this were a book about fun, you might expect me to talk about the science of fun, the history of fun, the value of fun, and the philosophy of fun. I'd create an elaborate equation on a quantum level: "If you take the square root of the song 'Don't Stop Believing,' divide it by the cosine of a slice of pizza, and multiply that by ceaseless childhood wonder, you become a fun person."

You'd probably also expect me to be a corporately appropriate pseudocomedian with wacky ties and a synergistic attitude. But this isn't that kind of book. And I'm not that kind of guy.

This is a book about action—less about learning, more about doing. Yes, you and I will occasionally dip our toes into the research behind how having fun helps make you more productive and more successful. We'll even brush up against how fun can help you be happier. But in the end, this is a book about helping you make having fun a necessary part of your daily routine.

As a coach of leaders, I've spent years consulting with hundreds of individuals and training hundreds of thousands of people worldwide via events and videos. During that time, I've come to believe that taking action on knowledge is far more powerful than just having knowledge itself. In fact, learning something and then not acting on it is often educated failure.

Intelligent, hardworking people have gone to great lengths to conduct brilliant studies and wonderful research experiments. That information has value. Ultimately, however, I'm less concerned with an experiment attempted by someone else and more concerned with an experiment conducted by you.

That's where this book comes in. I've designed it to be something like a private coaching session between you and me. Imagine that we're sitting across from each other in your office. My goal is to help you unlock the power of having fun. It's something that so many of us want to do, yet we forbid ourselves from doing it. I find that, for bizarre and occasionally sadistic reasons, far too many of us deprive ourselves of having fun. Yet the very thing that we prevent ourselves from doing is the very thing that can help us be more successful. Fun and work are not opposites. In fact, they are two sides of the same coin. Your work life and your personal life are inseparably connected.

Don't just take my word for it. After all, a book is just words on a page. The power lies in what you do with the information you acquire. That's my goal: to help you do something about having more fun in your day. I'll make it easy and, yes, fun for you to experiment. But please experiment. Your day, your time, and your activities are the laboratory. You and I will put on our lab coats and pocket protectors and put your experiment into action.

Sound good? Great! Just a little more housekeeping . . .

My hope is that this book has value for anyone in pretty much any position or stage in their career. However, the people who are going to get the biggest bang for their book buck are those who have some degree of flexibility when it comes to their work schedule. In this hypothetical coaching-via-book situation, my assumption will be that I'm talking to someone who has some ability to control how they spend their time.

In other words, if you're at the C-level, on salary, a free-lancer, a business owner, an entrepreneur, or even a stay-at-home mom or dad, you have the greatest opportunity to get the greatest value from this book. Why? Simply because a significant part of the experiment that you and I will be conducting has to do with crafting your schedule.

If you don't fit into one of these categories, if you are earning an hourly wage, or if you are working two or three jobs at present, you might find the execution of some of these principles a little trickier. Yet, if you still dare to continue reading this book despite being in one of those situations, you will still find value. I'd recommend that you approach this book with the mindset "How does this apply to me?" as opposed to "This doesn't apply to me." Read with an open mind, experiment where you can, and I believe you'll still uncover an empowering message.

Let's start experimenting with *The Power of Having Fun*!

Part One

The Desert and the Oasis

CHAPTER 1

Lost in the Desert

Consider the tales of two executives . . . well, three.

Story One: Businesscraft

There was once a business owner. He was a young man growing a moderately successful business. He hired employees. He made the sales. He managed the managers. He processed the profits. And most of all, he hustled . . . hard.

So hard, in fact, that when he invited me to provide some productivity coaching, it was clear that he was on his last leg. He was dragging himself through roughly *eighty* work hours per week. When I first heard that number, my CEO-coach-Spidey-sense began tingling. Putting it bluntly, I'm of the belief that any person who works more than sixty hours per week just simply does not know how to manage time—regardless of how productive they believe they are.

We did a deep dive. We accounted for every lunch break, meeting, phone call, nook, and cranny. Was time management a problem? Of course. But deep within the recesses of this man's schedule was a secret I was not expecting.

He was a paragon of the community. People flocked to him seeking guidance. He was well liked and had many important friends. His employees respected him. His competition feared him.

Yet he felt guilty, unproductive, and just a touch hypocritical—because a full twenty hours per week were lost to a secret habit he worked hard to hide. His wife and children had no idea. He would become the subject of scorn and ridicule among his peers were they to find out. You see, roughly twenty of those eighty "working" hours were spent in another world . . .

. . . the World of Warcraft.

Each day, he spent hours on end wandering the cyber wilderness as a level 47 Shaman because, in the real world, he was emotionally, mentally, and physically exhausted. He felt that he continually had to keep up appearances for his family and employees. Yet his desire to play caused him to jump in and out of the mists of Azeroth throughout the day to do battle with humans and orcs—then jump back into his business to haggle with suppliers.

When he made his confession to me, he hung his head. He knew he'd been caught. He expected me to tell him it was time to grow up, get focused, and behave as a good business owner should.

Story Two: Power Couple

Next is the story of two executives. They were a married power couple who worked in the same company. They were highly successful in their respective careers.

Together, they were a force to be reckoned with. She excelled in management and marketing. He was a wizard at the technical and financial details. They were a match made for the cover of *Fortune* magazine. They completed each other, professionally speaking, and they had me at "Hello, will you help us?"

Their relationship outside of work was going stale. Technically speaking, this couple worked a reasonable number of hours each week, meaning they left the office at a reasonable time. The problem was that they never really clocked out because when they got home, every conversation was about work.

Tuna casserole for dinner? Let's talk sales strategy.

Date night? Action items for the upcoming marketing campaign.

Changing the baby's diaper? Reevaluate current employee output.

While I helped them on the productivity side, we uncovered a deeper issue that needed resolution. Because a company is a reflection of its leadership, the couple's lack of balance in their personal lives had begun to be reflected in the lives of their employees. Like their fearless, well-qualified leaders, employees had become drained and were losing enthusiasm for the company.

Because this couple was unable to connect with each other outside of work, not only was their marriage at risk but the business as well.

Defining the Desert

What do these stories have in common?

Both occurred in a metaphorical desert.

If you've ever seen a desert epic, such as *Lawrence of Arabia*, you'll recognize that, sooner or later, someone's going to have to walk a very, very long way to get from one side of the desert to the other.

Man, I hate those scenes. If you're like me, you just can't wait for them to end. Look, I get it, Peter O'Toole is thirsty. Give him a Vitaminwater or cut to the next scene.

This perhaps overused desert trope is symbolic of many struggles in our lives, isn't it? Nothing comes easy. In spite of adversity, we need to keep pressing forward for what we desire because, despite the obstacles, we can make it! Hard work and perseverance are rewarded! Play a fanfare! Start the parade! Hail the conquering hero!

So, what's your desert today?

When I say *desert*, I have a specific definition in mind. A *desert* is how I'll refer to an extended period of deprivation and/or chaos in your life.

What is something that you're pushing yourself through? What's a situation for you that's slow and painful, where you're ignoring the signs that life is giving you to slow down or stop? Where are you putting up with extended periods of chaos because you're in such a hurry to get to the other side?

Before you attempt to answer these questions, it might be helpful to explore some possible deserts. Often, we carry our own deserts with us. What do I mean? In coaching executives and managers around the world, I've come across several deserts people carry on their backs as they live life.

THE RETIREMENT DESERT

Many people relentlessly push themselves in careers they hate just to reach the glorious shores of retirement. All the years and stress they put in will finally pay off. Someday, maybe, everything will be great, right? You can finally buy that RV you've always wanted and drive across the country. Or maybe you'll just live on a cruise ship in perpetuity—just one more slice of cheesecake . . . I don't want to be too full for shuffleboard this afternoon!

In the meantime, there's a lot of misery for a lot of folks. A study conducted by Harris and the University of Phoenix found that 59 percent of American workers wish they were in a different career. For those in their thirties, the number of disenchanted employees bumps up to 73 percent.

This news wouldn't be so bad if most people were truly building toward a healthy end-of-desert retirement plan. Yet they aren't. Per a GOBankingRates study, one-third of all Americans have absolutely zero in retirement savings, and 56 percent have less than $10,000 saved. How long of a postcareer retirement will that afford you? Which brings up our pal inflation, humming along on average at just over 3 percent. Not too bad, right? Until you consider that a paltry 3 percent increase means prices more or less double every twenty years.

THE ENTREPRENEURIAL DESERT

For some, such as entrepreneurs and corporate executives, reaching the other side of the desert may be cashing out. You sacrifice your time, health, sleep, and occasionally a relationship or two so that a glorious harvest will occur when Microsoft or Google or some other large company comes in and buys you out. With a small percentage of the proceeds, you could buy your own private island, a sports car, and a football franchise. Perhaps *Shark Tank* will cast you as one of the new "sharks." You'll be on TV and the cover of *Inc.* magazine. Your name will be synonymous with luxury and opulence, like a boss.

Unfortunately, exit rarely happens the way you might

think. Most business owners admit to me that they don't reach the exit they intended in the beginning, and—if they created a vision several years ago—they are currently nowhere close to realizing it. Yet they continue to sacrifice health, credit, and relationships on the altar of their businesses, hoping to appease the tribal deities of Musk, Zuckerberg, and Bezos, who may smile upon them and bestow a bounty of wealth.

THE PERSONAL DESERT

Others carry a much more personal desert with them. For some, reaching the other side may be when their children move out. I'm a father, and I love my kids dearly. However, I also know the sweet morsels of freedom that my wife and I enjoy when the little monsters are out of the house for an hour or two. Heck, just keeping the house clean for more than twelve minutes at a time would be a blessed occurrence. Am I right? If that's your idea of a good time, then you might be a parent.

Kids are certainly not the only personal challenge. Others might feel the other side of the desert is when they get married, or when they get divorced, or when they graduate from college, or when they can finally quit physical therapy, or when they work up the courage to ask someone on a date. Your desert might be just making it through the workweek so that you can party on Friday! The list is endless.

WHAT THE DESERT IS NOT

To clarify, hard work is a good thing. We should not be afraid of effort but embrace it. Effort helps us grow and makes us stronger for the coming years. There's even some joy and happiness to be found in an honest day's work.

One of my favorite quotes about work comes from an

unlikely source. Former US president Richard Nixon isn't remembered fondly for many things—perhaps rightly so—yet I respect him for saying, "To write a novel, you need an iron butt." Brilliant. Nothing crooked about that statement.*

In other words, if you're going to write a book, you need to put your butt in the chair and stay there until it gets done. I quite literally schedule "iron butt" time in my calendar when I set aside time to write. In addition to the mental demand, writing is also a test of maximal gluteal fortitude.

To do whatever it is you do, you need an iron *something*. Need to do those taxes? You also need an iron butt. Need to go out and make sales door to door? Iron legs. Creating a new proposal? Iron fingers and an iron mind. Kissing booth for charity? . . . You get the idea.

Hard work by itself is not a desert, yet it can quickly become so if we aren't vigilant. When we work as long as it takes to get the job done, when we keep pushing past the emotional and mental dehydration and deprive ourselves of necessary replenishment, we are building a life and career that are less likely to be successful.

Continual deprivation creates deficiency. Enduring chaos engenders fatigue. And, as the great coach Vince Lombardi said, "Fatigue makes cowards of us all." This is the desert we're targeting in this chapter.

Taking Your First Actions

Let's pause for a moment. After all, this book is a private coaching session, with me acting as your coach. Every once in a while, you're going to see an image like this:

---

*Maybe Nixon would've stayed out of trouble if he'd spent more time playing with the family dogs. Just sayin'.

• •

This icon is called an *Oasis Action*, and it means your coach wants you to do something with what you just read. Stop, take a moment, and do something quick, such as answer a brief question. By doing this, you'll not only gain knowledge from this book but also make positive changes starting today.

Here's your first action. Ready?

• •

List any desert(s) you're currently experiencing. If you have a hard time thinking of any, list deserts you've experienced in the last year or two:

1. _____

2. _____

3. _____

4. _____

5. _____

Next, write down the other side of each of these deserts. In other words, what is the end condition at which you'll know the desert is over?

1. _____

2. _____

3. _____

4. _____

5. _____

Did you do it? If you didn't do it, did you at least think deeply about your answers? Remember, this book is about the experiment of *you,* so the more involved you get in this process, the more valuable the book will become.

Let's continue. Whatever the other side of the desert means for you, the happiness that comes from reaching that glorious moment hides the dark and ugly reality that—between now and the other side—there's only:

Barren, dry land.

Buzzards.

Sun-bleached skulls.

Oh, sure, there are glimpses of hope here and there—a watery hunk of cactus or a Burning Man attendee, if you will. And that hope of reaching the end keeps you moving forward.

This desert mindset can be summed up in what I call the Culture of WISH:

WORTH

IT

SOMEDAY,

HOPEFULLY

Someday, all this effort will pay off. Someday, I'll feel better. Someday, I'll be happy. Someday, I'll have the success I deserve. Someday, we'll be able to be close as a couple again. Someday, I'll be able to focus on my children. Someday, I'll take that trip with my friends. Someday, I'll get a raise. Someday, I'll learn how to use chopsticks. Someday, I'll go for a Sunday drive. Someday, I'll take kickboxing lessons. Someday, bloody someday.

But in the meantime? Thirst. Frustration. Work. Stress. Lack of sleep. Anxiety. Being bombarded by a hundred demands simultaneously. Constantly putting out fires. Feeling the continuous pressure to stay ahead of the curve. After all, you never know who's going to come along and kick you out. Then, before you can shout "Time-out," there goes your hard-earned nest egg.

Sounds fun, right? Who wants to sign up for that ride?

Apparently, most of us. It's the way the system was set up, wasn't it? Dig in, endure, and push past the pain—that's the way we get the best results, right?

What if I told you that wasn't true? What if the Culture of WISH is, in fact, the pathway to less success? What if enjoying life now—today—in reality *increased* the likelihood of achieving success someday in the future? What if, by putting fun first, everything you do would be more productive?

That is the great experiment we're about to test together. Your work—no matter what it is—can and should pay off now. This month. This week. Today.

It's time for us to make the desert bloom—from the first step until your triumphant arrival at the other side.

CHAPTER 2

Building Your Oasis

Remember the two stories I began with? Let's return to them to hear how they turned out. The envelope, please!

Businesscraft: Part Two

The young business owner was slumped in his chair, defeated by a natural 20 roll by his business coach wielding the +1 sword of truth.

"You're going to make me stop playing Warcraft aren't you?" he muttered in defeat.

"No, I'm not going to tell you to stop." I then asked, "Is it necessary for you to play these games? Does taking a break to jump into the game help you have a clear mind for work?"

"Yeah, it does, actually."

"Then I'm not going to tell you to stop. I'm going to tell you to schedule it."

After much discussion and some debate, we settled on five hours a week being a far more appropriate amount of time. This schedule allowed him to play in a focused way, slicing and dicing warlocks with ease. He scheduled one hour at the end of each day, *before* he went home. These virtual battles gave him the ability to clear his mind of the day's real-life business battles. He could then focus his attention on enjoying his time with his family.

Overall, he dropped his work hours from eighty to fifty-five, including World of Warcraft time, and became far more productive on a weekly basis. He was more relaxed at work because he knew his outlet awaited him at the end of the day, and his relationship with his family improved.

Power Couple: Part Two

The couple pleaded for guidance. They were desperately trying to pull themselves out of their business-first marriage.

"What's something you both really enjoy?" I asked them. "What's something you could do together that would pull your attention away from work, even if it's just for an hour or so?"

Without speaking, they looked at each other as if to say, You tell him. No, you tell him!

Finally, the wife volunteered, "Well, we both like *Survivor.*"

"The reality show?"

"Yes," she muttered.

Energized, I replied, "Great! Let's create an appointment for the two of you to make sure you watch *Survivor* together."

To you, that may seem meaningless, but to them, it was everything. Not only did the couple enjoy a group of fake castaways navigating physical challenges and sabotaging each other all in the name of staying on a TV show for another week, but the show gave them something to talk about other than the day-to-day chaos of running a business.

This simple act of having fun—mutually agreed upon and mutually scheduled—quite literally turned their marriage around.

The Culture of WIN

The Culture of WISH teaches you that hard work, at any cost, is the pathway to success. By making our efforts "worth it someday, hopefully," our society is becoming dragged down, burned out, and bummed out. Some of us have reached a constant state of pathos. This may be one reason for the proliferation in recent years of books about happiness.

Thankfully, there is a surprisingly simple yet effective antidote to the Culture of WISH. We must make your effort worth it *now*. Not just sometime this week or later today, but right now.

This is the Culture of WIN:

WORTH

IT

NOW

Don't worry. I won't be in acronym mode for the rest of this book.* But this simple construct provides the antidote to "someday, hopefully." When you transition to the Culture of WIN, you are creating not just a career but a life that is "worth it"—so to speak—right now. Today. Not just at the end.

Return with me to our metaphorical desert for just a moment. As rough and dry and nasty as a journey like this can be, imagine stumbling upon a beautiful oasis. Dehydrated, exhausted, sunburned, and pushed to the edge of sanity, you are met by a sudden yet welcome vision of a sparkling blue pool, palm trees shading a soft cabana, and fruit juice and ceviche by the truckload. Best of all, it is not a mirage. It is real. Such an experience would refresh your soul, would it not?

---

* After all, I'm not Gary Busey.

When you're stranded in an endless desert, an oasis becomes a powerful ally. There's a reason why they have historically been epicenters of trade, essential pathways to weary travelers, and battlegrounds for regional control.

Some people stumble across their oasis from time to time. A party bus in Ibiza here, an ice cream social there, a brief trip to YouTube-land. Sometimes, people try to furtively sneak these moments in between this email and that call.

How do many people feel when they have innocent fun? Guilty! The Culture of WISH tells us we don't deserve such moments. It whips us out of our temporary paradise and back to crawling beneath the blistering sun.

Deserve is an undermining word because it implies good behavior earns you a reward. The Culture of WISH uses it to keep us under its grimy thumb. You don't deserve a break yet because you didn't complete that project. You don't deserve to have a little fun because everyone else is working. You don't deserve it because of the psychological baggage of your past.

The Culture of WISH is lying to you.

Pop quiz: If you're wandering through the desert, is water something you deserve . . . or is it something you need?

Unlike the WISHy-washy culture, the Culture of WIN recognizes that these moments of refreshment are an essential part of the journey. Just as you require water to make it across the desert, so also does your day require meaningful, refreshing, and fun breaks.

How essential are they? We'll cover a variety of evidence in this book, and here is a taste to wet your whistle. A study by the *Harvard Business Review* and the Energy Project found that when a supervisor encouraged team members to take regular breaks, employees were 81 percent more likely to stay with the company and had a 78 percent increase in their sense of healthiness and well-being. Additionally, those who took breaks at least every ninety minutes reported a 40 percent increase in creative thinking and a 28 percent improvement in focus. Who doesn't need that?

The Culture of WIN is about you taking control of your workday. You must claim the benefits of having little moments of fun not because you deserve them but because you know your performance will improve because of them.

The Oasis Strategy

The Culture of WIN, then, is about scheduling these refreshing moments first and making our enjoyment a top priority. Everything else must flow around them.

Think of this strategy as planning the entire desert journey, start to finish, and knowing ahead of time that you will need to discover small oases along the way. Every few miles or so, you can refresh yourself, replenish your reserves, and gain greater strength to continue onward to your final destination.

In this book, I'm going to regularly refer to creating your *Oasis* or *Oases.**

An Oasis represents a moment that *you* create. It is not something the self-proclaimed conference experts nor a ruggedly handsome, superbly charismatic author-speaker-business coach tells you to create. No. *You* will create the minutes that make all your effort worth it today.

An Oasis sums up whatever you define as a meaningful break. It's an analog I had to create in place of a word that doesn't exist in the English language. Think of it as a moment of fun, play, enjoyment, reward, fulfillment, refreshment, recharging, and chillaxing all rolled into one tasty tidbit.

---

*Weird plural, isn't it? You'll get used to it, though. Promise.

Your Oasis is a powerful tool—not just to give you happiness, but for getting more done in your day. Believe it or not, my clients who establish fun moments for an Oasis become more productive and more successful because they feel that the work is worth it now.

The more work you intend to do, the more valuable and vital the Oasis is. The type of Oasis you choose is up to you, yet you must take these breaks to achieve your best performance. Make the Oasis a part of your routine, and your work today will be not only more enjoyable but more effective.

Our goal is to preschedule and predetermine specific times of the day, week, month, and year when you enjoy these Oases.

To be done first. Up front. In advance.

Not when you have time in your schedule or if you get your work done, but because you have the time scheduled, just as you would an appointment with a VIP. Which is, in fact, true because the VIP just happens to be you.

To give you a picture of how this works, let's imagine a person stuck in the desert of retirement. The Culture of WISH would tell that person that this is what a proper career path should look like:

The Culture of Wish

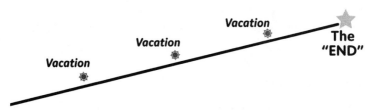

The philosophy? One big payout at the end—retirement—interspersed with a few well-deserved vacations. Yes, there's that "deserve" word again.

The Culture of WIN, on the other hand, would say that a career should be a steady flow of joyful moments:

The Culture of Win

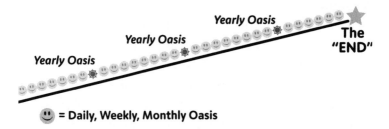

In this way, Oases become an essential part of how this person lives every day, week, month, and year. They become the top priority in daily and weekly planning. They are a requirement.

Regardless of the desert you find yourself in, the itinerary of your Oasis-filled journey should look like this: work hard for a short period of time and then take a small, refreshing Oasis. Repeat. Repeat. Repeat.

You take these Oases not because you are exhausted but because they are vital to your happiness and well-being. When you come back, you'll have enough in the tank for even more success. These Oases become one of the most—if not *the* most—important moments of the day.

Allow me to clarify a bit more. What are these Oases all about? What does—and doesn't—constitute an Oasis?

AN OASIS IS A TOP PRIORITY

To start, an Oasis isn't what happens at the end of the day. It's a critical part of the day. Your success is as dependent on taking this little break as it is for you to meet deadlines and respond to emails. Perhaps more so. As we dive into the concept of permission, you'll discover a little science behind the importance of having fun.

As you read further, I'm going to make the case for how businesses should create policies that allow employees to take these brief, inexpensive, and frequent Oases in the middle of the workday. If these breaks become an integral part of how people work, we will achieve greater performance as a result.

AN OASIS IS SCHEDULED

An Oasis doesn't happen out of the blue or whenever you need it. It is a scheduled daily occurrence. An Oasis is not a rescue inhaler that you use at the first sign of possible life congestion.

Let's be honest: when do we have time for anything, anyway? Ever tell yourself you're going to do something "when you have a moment?" How does that work out for you? Probably the same as for everyone else: a pile of actions left undone.

We can't afford to treat our Oases that way. In the twenty-first century, we never have enough time. Because that's the world we live in, it is important that we schedule time in advance to take these Oases in our day. We must make them a regular, recurring part of our schedule. That will make it much easier for us to stick to them.

AN OASIS IS A PRE-WARD

An Oasis isn't a reward. It is a *pre*-ward. See what I did there?

An Oasis is not a Milk-Bone offered as a reward for rolling over, playing dead, and being a good dog. Oases are necessary motivators to help you move forward. By *pre*-establishing and *pre*-scheduling these motivators in your day, you will feel a desire to work harder because you know something good is going to happen.

This serves as an alternative to working hard in the hope

that some supervisor might step down from the clouds of Olympus to bestow a gift upon you. This is not a gift that someone else gives you. It's something that you give yourself up front.

AN OASIS IS A WANT-TO

An Oasis is not a "have to" type of activity; it is a "want to" type of activity. Sometimes, people get confused when I introduce the concept of Oases, immediately thinking that they should be activities akin to running a marathon or eating whole-grain sprout sandwiches. Look, if those are things that you get excited about and look forward to in your day, they very well can be Oases. Kudos to you, you wonderful freak of nature.*

For the rest of us mortals, Oases are far more tangible and immediately gratifying. I find it more common for people to be excited about watching a show on Netflix, listening to a favorite song, or just walking in the park with their dog. We'll get into the details of creating Oases a little bit later. For the moment, understand that these are actions that you love to do, not need to do.

AN OASIS IS AFFORDABLE

Oases are not expensive. They are free to cheap.

Occasionally, people throw up a defensive wall around the Oasis concept because they feel as though I'm asking them to hurt their chances at that which truly is "worth it in the end." Right? "Dave's telling me to go on exotic vacations and travel six months of the year while other people do all the work for me. But that will kill my retirement plans." That's a different book, sold by someone with quite a different philosophy.

---

*Secretly, I'm jealous of you.

In reality, with the system I will teach you, you are going to be spending very little money. Instead, you'll make careful choices about Oases that are free or very inexpensive that give you pockets of joy. As we explore the process together, you may be surprised at how many joyful things there are that cost absolutely no money.

AN OASIS IS OFTEN BRIEF

An Oasis needn't be time-consuming. It can be brief. When I talk about setting up a daily win, a client will occasionally say, "Dave, I've got a department to run. I have responsibilities to fulfill and deadlines to meet. Time is money, and money doesn't grow on trees." They rattle off these business clichés as a defense mechanism, thinking I'm asking them to sacrifice time. No, that's the way of the Culture of WISH.

Little do they know how little time commitment is truly needed. It takes only a few minutes scheduled into your day to give you a breather and a moment of fun.

AN OASIS IS DOABLE

Oases are not goals. They are activities. When someone sets a goal, they're usually looking for the light at the end of the tunnel. Something distant.

For an Oasis to be worth it, it must also be a do it. Enjoying an Oasis is a matter of action. In most cases, Oases will take little effort.

Now, these Oases may improve, get more interesting, get more challenging, get a little weirder, or, heck, become downright goofy sometimes. What, where, and how you take your Oases is up to you. What is important is that you are doing them and doing them starting today.

AN OASIS IS FULFILLING

Oases are not self-indulgent; rather, they are self-*fulfilling*.

True confession? I was extremely hesitant about using the word *fun* in the title of this book because people occasionally equate fun with activities that are self-destructive. If you've ever been forced to watch *My Strange Addiction*, you know that certain behaviors offer a moment of pleasure but have a long-term negative impact. Heaven knows I don't want to show up at your intervention having to tell you how sorry I am for turning you into an online shopaholic.

So, here's clarification about the kind of fun that truly gives you power. This flavor of fun—these Oases—are things that help you feel happy and help you feel joy and fulfillment, but never in a way that creates a negative impact on you or the people around you.

An Oasis is constructive, not destructive. Sometimes this is a matter of degree. A client once told me she wanted to enjoy a little chocolate each day for her Oasis. That worked for her. However, if food as a reward has possible negative consequences in your life, you won't want to use it as an Oasis. This applies not just to food but to any other kind of activity that has a potentially negative, destructive side effect in your life. Choose options that build you up and make you a better person.

Now that we're on the same page with what an Oasis is and isn't, let's take a bird's-eye view of where you're at, right now, in terms of having fun.

CHAPTER 3

Your Fun Scorecard

$$\alpha\left(g^{is}\overline{w'^j}\frac{T'}{\overline{T}} + g^{js}\overline{w'^i}\frac{T'}{\overline{T}}\right)\left(\nabla_s\Phi + \frac{D\bar{u}_s}{Dt}\right)$$

$$\nabla_s[\bar{\rho}u'^s w'^i w'^j + (g^{is}w'^j + g^{js}w'^i)P' - w'^i\sigma^{js}(u') - w'^j\sigma^{is}(u')]$$

$$^{i'}w'^j\nabla_s(\bar{\rho}u'^s) - P'(g^{is}\nabla_s w'^j + g^{js}\nabla_s w'^i) = -\frac{1}{\bar{\rho}}\left[\sigma^{is}(u')\nabla_s w'^j + \sigma^{js}(u')\nabla_s w'^i\right]$$

= HAVE FUN

When it comes to having fun, how are you doing?

This is sort of an odd question, isn't it? Most people, if cornered by Katie Couric on the street, would respond by saying they are a "fun" person. However, I'm less interested in how fun or interesting or funny you are and more interested in how effective you are at having fun on a consistent basis. First, let's examine the three distinct kinds of Oases that we want to measure.

The Three Oases

You've likely heard of work-life balance, right? It's all the rage these days! It's the belief in a healthy relationship between hours spent in the workplace and hours spent outside work.

For this book, I'm more interested in your *Oasis balance*. This is the idea that you want to have a healthy amount of fun in three aspects of your life: personal, family, and work. Think of it as a three-legged stool, with all the legs evenly bearing the load of your massive Oasis strategy.

The *Personal Oasis* is all about you making time for yourself. Are you carving out enough time in your schedule to have some fun outside working hours and away from everyone else? When you've been thinking of having fun, if you're thinking about "me time," you've been viewing it in terms of the Personal Oasis. However, understanding it  and living it are two different things. I'll address assembling your Personal Oases in part two of this book.

The *Family Oasis* is about spending time with the people you love—and who love you—most. This includes anyone that you consider a close friend or relative. Your spouse, children, fiancé, boyfriend/girlfriend, brothers/sisters, mom/dad, and even your pet Fluffy can all fit into this category, as long as you feel a close connection to them. They need the power that comes from dedicated, focused time that you spend having a little fun with them. Part three of this book is dedicated to the Family Oasis.

The *Work Oasis* is how you go about taking little, meaningful breaks during your normal work schedule. Whether you work in a multinational behemoth with tens of thousands of employees or you're a stay-at-home parent, the Work Oasis is vital to your productivity. Most often, these are micro-Oases that occur a few times in each workday, although occasionally you or your company may make room for some bigger pauses from the day-to-day hustle. While leaders of companies and midlevel managers can do a lot to make these happen, most of the responsibility for creating a Work Oasis rests on the shoulders of each individual worker. Part four of the book is where we'll tackle the Work Oasis.

In my experience, when it comes to the Oasis balance, most people are deficient in one or more areas. They may be fantastic when it comes to being with their family, yet clueless about making time for themselves. They may have a great strategy for taking breaks at work, yet at home, it's a never-ending barrage of taking kids to practice, picking up the laundry, shopping for groceries, mowing the lawn, taking the dog to the vet, and getting a meatloaf in the oven before anyone realizes they are hungry.

All three legs of the stool must be firm and balanced. How are you doing in this department? Enter the Fun Scorecard.

The Assessment

This powerful little assessment is designed to gauge your key merriment metrics. Even if you're kicking back and reading just to get washed in words of wisdom—which may be a sign that you'll score well—I strongly recommend you pause, grab a pen, and take this fun little quiz. It shouldn't take you more than ten minutes and will gently guide you toward areas where you can make improvement.

You've got two options to get your Fun Scorecard:

Take it right here in the book, and I'll show you how to tally up your answers and interpret the results.

or

Take it online at **PowerofHavingFun.com/quiz**. There, you will find a friendly online version that will crunch the numbers for you and email you the results.

It's your call. Choose wisely.

HOW TO ANSWER

For each question, please circle the number that best represents how much that statement applies to you. For instance, 10 would be "You're darn tootin'!"; 5 would be "Meh, could happen. No promises"; and 1 would be "Nope."

Try not to overthink your answers. Just go with your first reaction to each statement.

Ready? Begin!

PART ONE: PERSONAL OASIS

Indicate how strongly you agree with these statements in terms of personal fun by yourself, with no one else present. Circle one number for each statement.

I can have fun by myself without feeling guilty.

1   2   3   4   5   6   7   8   9   10

I have a wide variety of options of fun things to do by myself.

1   2   3   4   5   6   7   8   9   10

I have a long-term personal hobby that I am passionate about.

1   2   3   4   5   6   7   8   9   10

Taking some "me time" is a top priority when planning my day or week.

1   2   3   4   5   6   7   8   9   10

My favorite personal fun activities are free or very affordable.

1   2   3   4   5   6   7   8   9   10

I am never too busy to take some fun time for myself.

1   2   3   4   5   6   7   8   9   10

I deeply enjoy the fun moments I spend by myself.

1   2   3   4   5   6   7   8   9   10

Total score for Personal Oasis _____ ÷ 7 = _____
average for Personal Oasis

What does this mean about your personal relationship with having fun?

1–4: Self-deprivation—You're likely experiencing a fun deficiency in your personal life. Those with these results typically sacrifice their personal fun for their loved ones, or their career, or both. Take care of no. 1 by deep diving into part two, "The Personal Oasis."

4.1–8: On the right track—There's a healthy amount of personal playtime in your day. You can fine-tune your fun time by learning more about the five stages of your Personal Oasis.

8.1–10: Living it up—You're regularly filling up your personal fun canteen with the essential reserves of enjoyment. Well done! Word of warning: Be careful that your definition of fun is healthy and appropriate. Keep your activities refreshing, fulfilling, and affordable.

PART TWO: FAMILY OASIS

For best results, choose the one family member or friend you feel closest to at this moment.

My closest family member or friend: _____

Now circle the number that indicates how strongly you agree with each statement in terms of having fun with this individual.

I believe it's essential for me to spend quality time with this individual.

1   2   3   4   5   6   7   8   9   10

I feel that the time we spend together makes me more successful in life and at work.

1   2   3   4   5   6   7   8   9   10

When planning activities with this individual, I put their wishes above my own.

1   2   3   4   5   6   7   8   9   10

I have a recurring, scheduled date or planned activity with this individual at least once per week.

1   2   3   4   5   6   7   8   9   10

I never allow work or personal worries to distract me during planned fun time with this individual.

1   2   3   4   5   6   7   8   9   10

I am never too busy to spend some time having fun with this individual.

1   2   3   4   5   6   7   8   9   10

I deeply enjoy the fun moments I spend with this individual.

1   2   3   4   5   6   7   8   9   10

Total score for Family Oasis _____ ÷ 7 = _____ **average for Family Oasis**

Got your answer? Let's take a look at what it means:

1–4: Disconnected—Stuff just keeps getting in the way. Deep down, you likely recognize you're losing touch with this person, yet you're not quite sure how to get it back. Enter the five stages of the Power of Having Fun. The guidance you need can be found in part three, "Your Family Oasis."

4.1–8: Hanging out—You're spending time with each other, and you're both gaining some power from it. The power could be so much greater with just a little more attention to fun. Not only will you become closer to that person, but every aspect of your life will benefit as a result.

8.1–10: Thick as thieves—Like Batman and Robin and peanut butter and jelly, your combined force is one to be reckoned with. Nicely done! Be sure to give yourself some personal time as well. This will fill up your reservoir even more so that you have more to give to the one you love.

PART THREE: WORK OASIS

If you are self-employed or a full-time parent, answer the questions by thinking of yourself as a company of one person, acting as leader, supervisor, and employee at the same time.

My current position at work: _____

Indicate how strongly you agree with these statements in terms of having fun in your workplace. Circle one number for each statement.

The leadership of this company has a written plan or policy about taking breaks and having fun.

1   2   3   4   5   6   7   8   9   10

The leadership of this company sets a positive example when it comes to having fun.

1   2   3   4   5   6   7   8   9   10

Supervisors encourage team members to take consistent breaks.

1   2   3   4   5   6   7   8   9   10

Supervisors encourage me to stop work at reasonable hours and enjoy my personal life.

1   2   3   4   5   6   7   8   9   10

I take a brief break from work at least every ninety minutes.

1   2   3   4   5   6   7   8   9   10

I sincerely believe I am in control of my own happiness at work.

1   2   3   4   5   6   7   8   9   10

The culture of our workplace is one of having fun.

1   2   3   4   5   6   7   8   9   10

Total score for Work Oasis _____ **÷ 7 =** _____ **average for Work Oasis**

Finally, let's review what your score means:

1–4: Workplace wasteland—Work is much harder than it needs to be and far less productive than it could be. By making an effort to infuse consistent breaks for fun into your workday, you'll boost overall performance. Regardless of your current job title, you'll find meaningful action you can take in part four, "The Work Oasis."

4.1–8: Staying on the level—There's some positive fun happening in your workday. You're headed in the right direction as long as you don't let the unexpected chaos take over your calendar. Work on building a case for having fun by demonstrating how your performance improves when you take meaningful breaks.

8.1–10: Reaching the summit—Having fun isn't a problem in your workday. You're in rarified air by being able to work in a place like this. Congrats! Continue contributing to a culture that prioritizes results achieved above hours worked.

You now have your baseline Fun Scorecard for the three types of Oases. With the results in hand, you've got some perspective on where you have room to grow. Now it's time to connect that perspective with an overview of the five-stage process toward having more fun.

CHAPTER 4

The Five Stages

I remember watching *Mary Poppins* when I was a kid. Besides having the hots for Julie Andrews, I remember falling madly in love with the theme of the song "A Spoonful of Sugar."* The big takeaway from that song is that any task can be made less dreadful if we make it fun. Whether it's cleaning your room, training employees, or creating a two-hundred-page report, a spoonful of fun will make the task far more manageable.

So that's what we'll do ... you and me in your office, before I open my umbrella and fly to some other business.

Think your situation is particularly tough? I'll bet you I've had clients in far worse shape. And my guess? You'll find yourself loving this process. They were skeptical, too, but once they got in the groove, not a single one of them said, "I hate this." Instead, their response has been, "How have I lived my life for so long without doing this!"

---

*Okay, so maybe I'm exaggerating on the second part.

Consider one coaching client I've been working with for many years now. When we began the coaching process, she was clocking close to sixty hours a week and barely keeping her head above water with the multiple-location school she owned. She was frustrated. She was tired. She wasn't getting to where she wanted to go—plus she was ready to have another child. Being a mother was important to her, but she didn't see how she would have the time.

Now? She's working about twenty hours a week or less. She feels more fulfilled and happier than ever. And, over the course of us working together, she and her husband have had another child. I've seen this pattern occur several times with many of the executive women I've worked with.**

But how is this result achieved?

Establishing a lifetime of Oases is a five-stage process. Think of these as the far more pleasant alternatives to the five stages of grief. Each person is in a different part of their journey toward having fun. Your scores let you know to which stages you need to devote the most attention.

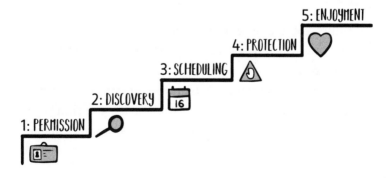

**In an earlier draft, I alluded to "being personally responsible" for the birth of dozens of children. This poor choice in wording caused my wife to object heartily, and the text was subsequently removed.

In parts two and three of this book, I dive into each of these stages in great detail. For the moment, here is a brief overview to let you know where we're headed.

Stage 1: Permission

Before you can start to have Oases, you must accept the fact that, hey, it's okay to have a little fun every now and then. No, it's better than okay, it's essential.

Permission is the stage that helps you acknowledge that having fun isn't just a good idea, it's absolutely necessary to your success. Not only does your brain need a strong grounding in the logic behind it, but your heart also needs to feel that establishing Oases is a pathway toward success.

Stage 2: Discovery

As adults, too many of us have forgotten how to enjoy ourselves. We're stuck in a perpetual cycle of sensible shoes and sensitive teeth.

Discovery is the stage in which you return to the wisdom you had when you were younger. You had a list of things you used to do for fun, but somewhere along the way, someone stole recess from you. The world is a sandbox—not a desert. Take back the playground.

Stage 3: Scheduling

The difference between idleness and recreation is a schedule. As mundane as it may sound, the power of having fun is unleashed when you plan for it.

Scheduling is the stage where you line up your adult responsibilities and then make fun a top priority. Oases shouldn't fill in the gaps in your calendar. Rather, they should become the industrial-strength super glue that holds your days, weeks, months, and years together.

Stage 4: Protection

Even with the best schedules, life can sometimes "life" us. But having fun should never be a casualty.

Protection is the stage at which we draw up a strategy to ensure that we are prepared for life's many obstacles. By inoculating yourself against challenges like guilt, apathy, and a constant state of busyness, you can ensure that having fun will provide the maximum benefit.

Stage 5: Enjoyment!

When fun happens, do you feel it? If you find yourself putting on a fake smile and telling yourself that it's almost over, it doesn't count.

Enjoyment is the stage where you strengthen your enjoyment muscle. For many, simply being in the moment is a lost art. You see it at every child's dance concert: a sea of people trying to capture a good shot of their little darling executing flawless jazz hands, while they miss soaking in the joy of simply watching her twirl. You can practice techniques that will fully engage your brain in fun activities. Then you'll more fully enjoy the benefits you receive from making that simple time investment.

Got the big picture? Time to put these five stages into practice, starting with your personal ability to have fun. Please take my hand, and let's jump into this chalk drawing together.

Part Two

The Personal Oasis

CHAPTER 5

Stage One:
Your Permission to Play

For a moment, imagine that you're nine years old. Your teacher is lecturing about the importance of long division or vowels. You're waiting for the hour hand on the clock to reach 2. You may still have a tough time reading analog clocks, but you know that the 2 means recess time. The time arrives, and, like a Tasmanian devil, you recklessly shove your school supplies into your desk and run out the door. For a solid fifteen to twenty minutes, you play foursquare, tag, follow the leader, make-believe, and—the mother of all recess games—kickball.

Different countries use difference words: recess, break, interval, playtime, free period, morning tea. Whatever you call it, the result and the meaning are the same: a necessary break for children from the rigors of schoolwork. The American Academy of Pediatrics has repeatedly emphasized that children need to have downtime between cognitive challenges. Even the Office of the United Nations High Commissioner for Human Rights has weighed in, recognizing the right for children to play as an essential part of their well-being.

Yet, oddly enough, many schools have greatly reduced recess or have eliminated it altogether. According to some studies, as much as 50 percent of American kids no longer have recess despite overwhelming evidence showing how it can improve performance. It would appear that the culture of the WISH-infected adult world has started to fester around our kids.

Consider the adult side of this issue: Americans are taking fewer vacations than ever. According to the Project: Time Off's 2016 report, nearly 55 percent of all Americans fail to use up all of their vacation time. This resulted in an estimated record-setting 658 million vacation days wasted that year.

If our goal were to be both joyless and productive, an argument could be made for never taking a vacation as adults or having recess as children. But it doesn't work. In fact, the same study found that employees who take ten or fewer days of vacation time are *less* likely to have received a raise or bonus in the last three years than those who took eleven days or more. In case that isn't obvious enough, forgive me as I make it perfectly clear:

When you take less vacation, you earn less money. When you take more vacation, you pave the pathway to promotion.

Someone didn't just steal recess from you. They robbed you of the very tool you need to be successful! Time to take it back.

Bringing Fun Back

I'd like to give you a license. No, not a license to drive a forklift or to kill like James Bond. This is your license to have fun, relax, and find refreshment. I, by the power vested in me, am giving you permission to enjoy yourself.

To make it official, there is a license in the back of the book for you to cut out and put in your wallet. Cheesy, yes. But also effective.

To earn this license, you'll need to do a little enjoyable homework first. After all, these are just words in a book. What authority does a book have? We need this license to mean more to you than just a cornball motivational poster of a kitten saying, "Hang in There, Baby." This isn't about telling you what you deserve. Remember, "deserve" is the desert mindset. The Oasis mindset is about what you really, truly, deeply need.

You *must* refresh and recharge your day. How you feel about life emotionally has a considerable biological impact on your daily performance. Don't believe me yet?

The Mini Experiment: Part One—Desert

Play along with me for a moment as we do an exercise together. Please do this rather than just read about it, as it will help you give yourself permission more quickly than by me lathering you up with study upon study. While it may seem silly, the result you get from this fun test has long-term implications for your productivity and success.

You'll need a pen and a timer of some kind—such as a stopwatch on your phone or the second hand on a clock. Got them handy? Let's begin.

• •

Write down a "desert" you're experiencing right now—whichever one is top of mind. Remember, a desert is an extended period of deprivation and/or chaos in your life. If you need help coming up with your desert, refer to the list you made back in chapter 1.

My desert is: _____

Now it's time to immerse yourself in that desert. Take it in. Get your stopwatch or timer ready.

For a full sixty seconds, imagine that desert. Describe in ten words or phrases how that desert makes you feel. Stop when you reach sixty seconds, even if you haven't completed the list. Ready? Go!

1. _____   6. _____

2. _____   7. _____

3. _____   8. _____

4. _____   9. _____

5. _____   10. _____

Now stop and immediately write down how much energy you have on a scale of 1 to 10, with 10 being an overcaffeinated Jim Carrey and 1 being a sloth with the flu.

My in-desert score: _____

Perfect. You've just allowed yourself to feel the full weight of that desert. If your score wasn't at least below a 7, odds are you didn't choose a truly challenging desert.* You may want to give it another go before moving forward.

The Mini Experiment: Part Two—Oasis Game

Now that you're feeling like a desert traveler, parched and perspiring, it's time we give you a mini oasis, or *MicrOasis*.

In this case, I'm going to give you three options for breaks you can choose from, with each being one minute in length.

First, decide which one of these three activities you want to perform. Don't spend a lot of time thinking about it. Go with your gut, follow the fear, and commit. Hard.

☐ **Option 1: The Balancing Pens Game**

How many pens can you balance on your face using just gravity? No props, no tape, no stuffing pens in your mouth.

Have an assortment of pens and pencils handy, and then start the timer. Place the pens on your face, one by one. Within the one-minute time limit, how many can you pile up on your face?

---

*Or, you may be the Unbreakable Kimmy Schmidt.

One woman was able to stack up more than twenty pens on her face during a live event I did. Can you beat her? If you can, get someone to take a picture and email it to me at **fun@DaveCrenshaw.com** or share it on social media with the hashtag **#PowerofHavingFun.**

☐ Option 2: The Pen-Catching Game

Only got one pen or pencil handy? No problem!

Place the pen on the back of your hand. Then, in one movement, flip your hand up in the air and catch the pen.

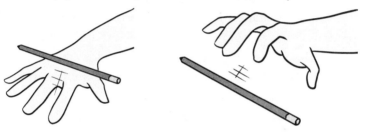

See how many times you can catch the pen within the sixty-second time limit. My personal best is thirty-four. Can you beat me?

☐ Option 3: Watch Funny Videos

Prefer something more passive and screen-oriented? Visit this page: **PowerofHavingFun.com/video**

There you will find a bunch of quick, funny videos curated from YouTube for a variety of tastes. All are safe for the workplace and children.

Set your timer for one minute. Watch. Stop when the timer goes off, no matter where you are in viewing.

Now that you've selected your MicrOasis, do it! Use the timer, and stop at sixty seconds.

Then, immediately after completing this one-minute activity, write down, on a scale of 1 to 10, how much energy you have, 10 being absolutely energized, and 1 being an industrial-sized vat of pudding.

My Post-Oasis Score: _____

Notice any change? If you deeply immersed yourself in the process of first thinking through the desert and then engaging in a harmless, mildly fun distraction, odds are you experienced a significant swing in emotions and energy—in just a matter of two minutes.

This illustrates the power that a brief, carefully chosen moment can have. Many of my clients have reported that a small ten-minute break to walk around the block or listen to their favorite song gives them all the energy and enthusiasm they need to work for the rest of the afternoon. Enjoying an Oasis within the desert of the workday is like going to a miniature carnival in your head.

A cleverly titled study, "A Walk Down the Lane Gives Wings to Your Brain," was published in *Applied Cognitive Psychology*. The authors, Steinborn and Huestegge, found that rest—vs. continuous work—improved performance. That's likely not a surprise to most people. However, they also discovered that the type of rest—whether active, such as taking a walk, or passive, such as watching a video—had essentially the same benefit. In other words, whether you go for a jog or veg out with YouTube, an Oasis recharges your internal batteries.

Let's couple that with a fascinating study with an unfortunate name: "The Role of Dopamine in Learning, Memory, and Performance in a Water Escape Task." Researchers from the University of Washington found that mice, when deprived of the naturally occurring, motivation-inducing chemical dopamine, took significantly longer to perform a simple task. The more they persisted in that task, the *worse* their times got.

On the other hand, mice that had a little pick-me-up of dopamine at any point in the process cut their performance time roughly in half.

We're not mice. Yet some of us are treating ourselves like a rodent in a maze, doomed to repeat the same experiment over and over . . . with no joy in sight.

But you can choose to inject a little fun in your personal lab experiment of performance.

The Culture of WISH says that you must work hard for long, extended periods of time, and only when work is "done"—which truthfully will never happen—do you deserve to experience success. This approach deprives the mind of dopamine for those extended periods of time, reducing motivation.

On the other hand, the Oasis mindset says that by working hard and taking enjoyable breaks on a repeated, regular basis, you will succeed more and experience greater success. You do this not because you deserve it, but because you need it and because it pushes you forward. My field experience coaching leaders around the world confirms this. I've seen, time after time, how little Oases yield big benefits.

In the back of the book, your License to Have Fun is waiting for you. It may seem like a small or even silly gesture. Yet in the moments when you feel you need to keep working, pushing—because that's what the Culture of WISH would tell you—pull out that License to Have Fun. Think of the many reasons why enjoying Oases are so vital to your success and happiness.

If you want, put your name on it, draw or paste on a picture of yourself, and add your favorite quote that will remind you that it's okay to have fun. If you're looking for a good quote, perhaps you can borrow a line from one of my favorite movies:

"Life moves pretty fast. If you don't stop and look around once in a while, you could miss it."

CHAPTER 6

Stage Two: Discovering Your Fun

Are you a list maker? Some people are masters at creating lists—they live for it. I dabble, but I don't delve. For instance, I occasionally play around with my list of top-five movie actors (Cumberbatch and DiCaprio are usually near the top). Or sometimes it's my favorite Coca-Cola Freestyle concoctions (Vanilla Sprite + Fanta Lime = key lime—try it, you won't be sorry). And, of course, there is my top-five song list for Jazzercise ("She's a Maniac" beats "Vogue" by a nose).

Pretty much all of us are familiar with the idea of the playlist. Whether it's Netflix or iTunes, we love filling up those lists with films and tunes that tickle our fancy. Building this list in advance makes it easy for us to sit down, relax, and enjoy at a moment's notice. However, listening to music or watching Netflix all day often fails to leave us feeling fulfilled.

Others, to bridge that gap of fulfillment, have created a bucket list—the semimorbid idea of listing things you'll do before you kick the bucket. Usually, these ideas range from the relatively mundane (visit Lichtenstein) to the downright dangerous (participate in the Running of the Bulls) to the just plain weird (go to a live taping of *The Price Is Right* dressed as Guy Fieri). However, the concept can sometimes leave people feeling that they're falling short. Why? Because they don't have enough money—or time—to complete these amazing activities, and often they get lost in the shuffle of living in the real world.

I'd like to introduce you to the Oasis List. It combines the simplicity of a playlist with the joy of a bucket list, but with zero guilt, little pressure, and little cost in terms of either time or money. Your Oasis List will be a list of small- to medium-size moments that bring a little fun, joy, relaxation, and recharging to your day. Not sure what I mean? To give you a taste, here's a list of potential ideas in order of increasing effort and cost:

Take a walk	Take a half-day off
Listen to music	Host a charitable event
Enjoy a nice lunch	Explore family history
Eat a bit of special candy	Get away for three-day weekend
Enjoy a long bath	
Watch TV	Relax at the spa
Play video games	Go on a date with children
Exercise	
Ride a motorcycle	Take an extended vacation
Volunteer at school	
Coach children	Make a major purchase
Get a massage	Finish the basement

Now, on this list, you'll notice that I've mixed in activities that involve other people in addition to yourself. Setting up Oases for people you care about is so essential that I'll cover that concept in its own section later in the book. But for now, please focus on ideas that are Personal Oases just for you.

Remembering Fun

How do we get started? At some point, someone must have asked you, "What do you like to do for fun?"

For a little experiment, the next time you're at any kind of mixer, ask people that question and see what response you get. Some people will, without hesitation, tell you something they're passionate about. Many people—increasingly more and more of us—have a hard time answering that question. Occasionally, people respond with what they think others want them to say. It's as if we've become so saturated with the Culture of WISH—of just working hard because it's only worth it in the end—that we have forgotten what gives us joy.

To help adults like you and me rediscover what's fun in our lives, I engaged Touchstone Research to conduct an exhaustive survey of children ages five through eleven. They came from all geographic areas of the United States and from a wide variety of cultural, racial, and socioeconomic backgrounds.

One question I asked them was: "Many adults work too hard and have forgotten how to have fun. What would you say to an adult who has forgotten how to have fun?"

As you can imagine, when you're grilling kids in this age group, you're going to get some pretty great stuff. Here are a few examples:

From an eight-year-old boy in California: "Just chill, chill, chill. Time to let it go and have fun, Daddy."

A five-year-old girl from the Midwest answered, "Be yourself and play with toys."

Another five-year-old girl said, "Come to play tea party with me and also watch funny cartoons. It helps me a lot, too."

A six-year-old boy from the South was detailed in his answer: "Play the Xbox with me, or let's go to the beach. I love the beach because you can make sandcastles, bury people in the sand, and go swimming and collect seashells. You have to use lotion or you will get burned." Valid point!

Now, it's not my intent when I share these quotations to encourage you to be childish. Adults should be adults. You don't need to sing along to the *Spongebob Squarepants* theme song whilst bouncing on a trampoline and drinking Hi-C out of a sippy cup. A few people may find that to be an Oasis, yet my guess is most would not.

Oases aren't about being child*ish* but about being more child*like*. What's the difference? One of the best traits children have is that they view the world with wonder. They find fun and play wherever they are, regardless of what they're doing or what resources they have. It's true that most kids are plugged in these days, and many will default to playing Minecraft if given the option. That said, based on my personal experience, if you give a child an empty field with a few rocks in it, eventually they will find a way to turn it into a playground. Children are *fun*preneurs.

This chapter contains a worksheet that is also included in the back of the book. For now, let's just do a brief walk-through of what this exercise is all about. In the first column, you'll see a variety of different ages: 10, 15, 20, and 25 plus. There are two simple columns that follow.

Age	What did you like to do for fun?	Why did you enjoy it?
10 years (Example)	*I liked playing with Legos*	*I enjoyed being able to create new things: Also playing pretend with friends and interacting between "characters."*
10 years		
15 years		
20 years		
25+ years		

In the example above, I wrote in that I liked playing with Legos. I wasn't Zack the Lego Maniac from the commercials in the '80s, but I was pretty darn close.

Why did I enjoy it? Well, I enjoyed being able to construct new worlds. I also loved using my Legos to play make-believe. I'd commission family and friends to play along as I created characters and told stories. I vividly remember developing an epic back story for the Lego Spaceman, the one with the cheesy helmet, torn between saving the world and keeping his relationship with his Lego space girlfriend. Yes, I know I was a bit overromantic as a child.*

I share this not to make the process about me but to offer an example of how to complete the worksheet. What is it that *you* used to like to do as a child? Need help remembering? Let's get some help from kids. In that survey of five hundred children I mentioned, we also asked them what makes them happy.

The following is a summary of their responses. Take a moment and scan through this list to see whether it reminds you of anything that you used to like in your youth.

Spend time/playing with family/friends

Read books

Watch TV/movies

Swim

Play with pets

Watch YouTube

School/learning

Ride bicycle/scooter

Go on vacations

Play video games

Play with toys

Eat food/ice cream

Play at the park/outside

Dance

Play board games

Listen to music

Play on phone/tablet

Play sports

Play with dolls/Barbie

---

*See reference to Mary Poppins in chapter 4.

Make art

Make jokes/laugh

Be good/make others happy

Eat candy/sweets

Share hugs

Use the computer/the Internet

Play card games

Ride horses/ponies

Sing

Play an instrument

Go to church

Do nails

Fashion/clothes/shop

Play superhero

Celebrations/holidays/birthdays

Read comics

Karate/Jujitsu

Climb

Bake

Skate

Explore nature

Cars/motorcycles

Hobbies

Act

Write

Invent

See pretty things

Enjoy a beautiful day

That's quite a list, isn't it? Did reading it stir up some ideas for you? Fun things you used to do, but somehow forgot?

In case you're interested in adult-generated ideas, here are some of the answers I received from nonchildren when I conducted a couple of straw polls on social media:

Meditate

Connect with people

Delicious food

The sound and smell of the ocean

Dance

Sing

Walk in nature

Feel a closeness with God

Garden

Spend time with children/grandchildren

Nap

Listen to inspirational speeches

Go for a swim

Go for a run

Camp

Bake/cook

Read	Watch a favorite
Sit outside in the	TV show
fresh air	Yoga
Create art	Go to a spa
Sports	Spend time with pets
Do genealogy	Go for a drive/ride

Now it's your turn.

Using the worksheet on the next page or in the appendix, create your initial brainstorming list of things you might like to do for fun. Use the above responses from children and adults as a guide. Create a random list of activities, in no particular order, that you might find interesting.

Next, you can categorize your list. Here's a worksheet to help you place them into one of five columns. These columns are simply organized according to how long each thing might take you to do, including a space for estimated cost.

Length (Category)	Activities	Estimated cost
(Example) Under 15 minutes (daily)	*Watch a fun video on YouTube for a few minutes*	*Zero*
Under 15 minutes (daily)		
15 to 90 minutes (daily or weekly)		
90 minutes to 12 hours (weekly or monthly)		
One half-day to 3 days (monthly or yearly)		
More than 3 days (yearly)		

In the Estimated Cost column, just write a ballpark figure. Obviously, going for a walk around the block is free. If you put down something more elaborate, like a long vacation, perhaps you should put in a few thousand dollars as the cost. Don't overthink it right now.

Take the list you created in the brainstorming exercise and transfer each activity that you would enjoy into the worksheet above. Categorize each idea according to the amount of time it would require. Then make a note about the estimated cost next to each activity.

Transferring the brainstormed list to an organized chart will make our next step easier: scheduling and committing to these Oases.

CHAPTER 7

Stage Three: Scheduling Your Oases

Have you got your Personal Oasis list? Great. The next step is to establish a schedule. In particular, we want to establish a pattern of recurring Oases that you will enjoy, regardless of what might be happening in work or in life.

Oases come first. This doesn't necessarily mean they are the first thing you do in the day. In fact, many of my clients enjoy their Personal Oases near the end of each day. "Come first" means they are scheduled as a top priority. You reserve time in your calendar for Oases, and everything else needs to fit around them.

The Daily Oasis

To get a feel for how this works, let's find the smallest, least expensive thing you put on your Oasis List from the last chapter. Look in the Daily column and find something easy, like five minutes of shadow boxing each day.

Scheduling time for this requires that you have a calendar you use regularly. Whether it's paper or digital doesn't matter. When in doubt, go digital; it will make this process easier for you in the long run.

Review your list and find a brief, free Oasis. Then schedule it into an open space for today or tomorrow.

You're not done yet because now you need to establish a recurring schedule for your daily Oasis, where it will occur almost every single day. I say almost because there are going to be exceptions—notably when you have a larger weekly, monthly, or yearly Oasis that occurs in place of your daily Oasis. For example, perhaps you scheduled a vacation as a yearly Oasis. In that case, if your vacation overlaps with your daily Oasis, that's fine.

But what exceptions are not acceptable? Those like attending a business conference, dealing with an extended home project, or even—heaven forbid it should happen—dealing with personal tragedy. This daily Oasis, remember, is a necessity. It is something that you must take every single day, regardless of what is happening. As we established in the chapter on permission, the Oasis gives you strength. It gives you energy.

Having trouble figuring out where to schedule this in your calendar? Pick the easiest time slot that you can imagine. Pick the time of day when you're least likely to have to switch your attention, when something is rarely going on—for instance, just before you go to work, after lunch, upon finishing work, or right before bedtime.

One of my CEO clients scheduled an appointment right after her lunch break every day. She literally added on her calendar, "Take a walk to visit my friend Bessie the cow." Her Oasis was to leave her office, walk up the hill to a local pasture, pet the cow on the nose, and then head back to work. For her, that recharged her batteries.

Personally, I take a daily Oasis every day at 4:30 p.m. What do I do? I play video games for thirty minutes.

Shocked? To some, this would not be refreshing. I, however, am a geek with a brain that is running so fast that it torments me constantly. Sometimes, the only thing that turns it off is to bust out a polygonal M2000 Super-Bazooka and pwn* noobs until I'm back to being even keel.

This Personal Oasis is about what works for you . . . no one else.

Right now, before you continue, take the following action:

∙∙∙

Either by repeating the Oasis you just scheduled or by creating a new one, schedule a recurring daily Oasis that is thirty minutes or less and is free or extremely inexpensive.

---

*No, it's not a typo. Google it.

Finished? Great job on taking your first step into Oasis-land!

The Necessity of Time Management

It's possible that you just ran into an issue, and that's the need for you to bring some time-management skills to this party. Establishing these Oases should dovetail nicely into any time-management system you're currently using.

But what if you're not currently using a system? What if your time management is in a bit of disarray? You might want to make that the next book you read or course you take.

There are many great time-management systems out there. Some ways of approaching time speak to certain kinds of people more than others. Use what you know and are familiar with, and you'll be able to succeed with the principles I share here about finding your Oases.

If you're uncertain about which program to use, or feel you are in need of a refresher, may I humbly suggest you take my time-management courses for a spin. Many people have reported that their lives and careers have improved significantly because of them.

Time Management Fundamentals is located on LinkedIn Learning (formerly known as Lynda.com). You can access it at **DaveCrenshaw.com/time**. LinkedIn Learning offers a free trial, which should give you more than enough time to complete my course as well as to evaluate whether the thousands of other courses justify the monthly investment.

The Weekly Oasis

Now let's create a weekly Oasis. The weekly Oasis is slightly more substantial and perhaps a little more of an investment—

though not necessarily. You're shooting for something around the sixty-minute mark. Take a look at your Oasis list to find something that grabs your attention. What's one thing that you'd like to do once a week that recharges your batteries and that you can take a little extra time doing?

One of my clients is a business executive who loves riding his Harley. He would schedule time each Friday to grasp the ape hangers of his majestic hog and ride free, like a man without a code searching for the next whistle-stop town to carve his initials in. And when he was done, he'd just go back to work. Refreshed. A rebel *with* a cause.

Time to take action!

• •

Review your list and find an Oasis that is around sixty to ninety minutes and fairly inexpensive. Then schedule it as a weekly recurring appointment with yourself.

How does that feel? Can you feel the slight bump in freedom and control that you just gained for yourself by doing this simple activity? You have now staked a claim in your day: a period of time that should not be touched by anyone but you.

Now, we're not quite done yet. You'll want to do an initial review of how successful and refreshing those Oases are for you.

· ·

Schedule a fifteen-minute appointment with yourself, approximately two weeks from now, to evaluate your daily and weekly Oases. In the notes for the appointment, put "Evaluate my daily and weekly Oases. Were they meaningful? Is there anything I would change about them?"

When the time arrives for that appointment, you're going to take a moment and consider your two starting Personal Oases. Do you still like them? When you kept those appointments with yourself, did they give you energy? Or did they not work out so well? Was the time allotted not quite right?

As you consider these questions, adjust your Oases—in terms of length, schedule, or activity—to make them more effective, and then reestablish them in your schedule. Once you get into a good rhythm, you won't have to reassess every two weeks. Most of my clients do this on a quarterly basis. However, to start, reassess your Oases every two weeks for a month or two. After some time, you can begin to be a bit more flexible, occasionally incorporating new items from your Personal Oasis list.

You're off to a great start! Now, let's think bigger.

Big-Time Oases

With the daily and weekly Oases, you've experienced a bite-size taste of fun and success. These little pick-me-ups will help you feel more motivated to work and succeed during the rest of the day and week. Now it's time to establish something more meaningful and substantial within your schedule. Monthly and yearly Oases include a celebration of the work you accomplished. They're a way for you to look back and give yourself a pat on the back for all the hard work you've put in.

Because they're more meaningful and substantial, these Oases also require more planning and, occasionally, additional investment. The key is to remember that Oases should always be affordable, both in terms of time and money.

Affordable in terms of time means you don't want to overcommit yourself to the point of stress or where you're neglecting work activities. Of course, you must get your work done. However, you can carve out enough time provided that you do it several weeks or several months in advance.

Affordable in terms of money simply means to choose Oases that are well within your means. As a rule of thumb, limit your monthly personal Oasis budget to roughly two times what you make per one hour of work. On the yearly level, limit your Oasis budget to no more than twelve times what you make per hour. In other words, if you make $30 per hour, you'll have about $60 for a monthly win and $360 for a yearly win. Keep in mind that this is a *Personal* Oasis, not a Family Oasis (like an extended vacation), which I'll cover in the next part of the book.

THE MONTHLY OASIS

Moving on, let's select an item from the Oasis List that lasts about a day or half a day. This might be creating a three-day weekend, visiting a spa, or painting an impressionistic masterpiece.

Select an activity from your Oasis List that would work for your monthly Oasis. Look for something that lasts a half-day to a full day and is well within your budget.

Got it picked out?

Now you're ready to schedule your first monthly Oasis. Pull out your calendar and scan the next four weeks. Where can you carve out a half day?

If taking *any* time off work is out of the question, then at least carve out specific hours of a weekend. For example, you might try from noon to 10 p.m. on the third Saturday as designated Personal Oasis time.

If fitting this into the next four weeks is too tricky, look at the following four weeks. Odds are, sometime in the next eight weeks, there's a space where, given enough advance notice, work and family will survive without you for a few hours.

Remember, you have a license to do this. If you are feeling unsteady about the reasons for having an Oasis, please refer back to chapter 5 regarding permission.

Schedule your first monthly Oasis to occur sometime within the next thirty days.

Now let's see if we can establish that monthly Oasis as a recurring appointment. It's best to choose a particular day of the week; for example, the third Thursday of each month.

This gives you a pattern that's repeatable, regardless of how the dates shift.

Creating this recurring schedule will be easy for some. For others, what they're being asked to do is a bit of a leap of faith. But trust me. By creating this schedule, you will become more successful. You will achieve more. You will have more energy. This is about necessity.

Either by repeating the Oasis you just scheduled or by creating a new one, schedule a recurring monthly Oasis that is one-half to a full day and is well within your budget.

You may find that you need to adjust this pattern over time; it's natural and occasionally necessary. If a conflict comes up that is unavoidable, it's okay to move your monthly Oasis. But the emphasis is on the word *move*, not *remove*. Never delete a monthly recurring Oasis. Only reshuffle it and keep it on the schedule. Give yourself about seven days of leeway to reschedule a monthly Oasis when absolutely necessary.

THE YEARLY OASIS

Now we're ready to move onto the granddaddy Oasis of them all—the yearly Oasis. Some people will think in terms of vacation. That's fine, just don't limit yourself.

For example, on a personal level, my Oasis is a fun and fancy tech upgrade tied to how much I made per hour that year. This allows me the freedom and absence of guilt to invest in something that I might normally not buy. For instance, I spent a chunk of change on the latest Xbox. You might think my wife would object to me buying something silly like that. However, remember that she's got her Personal Oasis as well. This kind of balance has worked well for my clients, too.

I'm guessing a video-game console won't do it for you, though. Many of my clients opt for an extended personal trip— an extended "me" vacation.

Take a look at your Oasis List and pick something that is substantial or lasts more than a few days. A trip someplace that you've always wanted; a purchase you want to make. Something like that. Keep in mind the rule of thumb for budgeting: spend no more than twelve times what you make per hour. This may not give you much room for going on a massive cruise somewhere or taking a six-week trip to Bora Bora. No, this may be more like going camping for a week, a four-day excursion to Six Flags, or maybe a cross-country trip on your road bike. Remember, this Oasis is about you. We will talk about taking family vacations later in the book.

Look forward into your schedule. Where in the next twelve months can you set aside a few days to enjoy this Oasis or go out and make this purchase for yourself?

Schedule your first yearly Oasis to occur sometime within the next twelve months.

After you've scheduled that Oasis, what next? Don't we want to establish recurring Oases like we did with the other time periods? Well, for practical reasons, yearly Oases often don't line up nicely like that.

However, you can create a reminder a couple of weeks after the yearly Oasis to start thinking about the next one. For instance, if you take a trip on March 15, you might create a reminder for March 29 to review how that Oasis went and to schedule the next one sometime in the next twelve months. Waiting a couple of weeks is good because it gives you time to relax and recover from the last yearly Oasis, yet it will still be fresh in your mind.

Schedule a reminder to review both your monthly and yearly Oases. For the best results, schedule this reminder two weeks after your yearly Oasis is set to occur. In that appointment, ask yourself the following questions: What did I like? What would I change? Too long? Too short? Budget?

Again, once you get into the rhythm of these Oases, you can begin to be more flexible. You remember all those other ideas that you put on your Oasis List? Over time, give them a try. There's some value in changing things around and spicing it up.

For now, just establishing the pattern is most important. By doing this, you're essentially forming a new framework for how you are going to live your life. It's such a simple, small thing but incredibly powerful. Despite all the power behind it, because it's fun, you can do it, and you will *want* to do it. And because you'll want your Oases, they'll be more likely to happen.

. . . Except when they don't.

CHAPTER 8

Stage Four: Protecting Your Oases

Wouldn't it be perfect if everything went according to the schedule you created? That by virtue of putting something on your calendar, it just happened and nothing got in the way? Wouldn't it be nice if life, work, and the kids just rolled over and accepted that having an Oasis is a top priority?

Yeah, good luck.

What we need is a just-in-case scenario that protects you from having these time slots tampered with—because they will get disrupted. Count on it.

However, we can inoculate you against these disruptions. Think about what a vaccination does. I, anticipating a lot of exposure to the world of bacteria and disease, preempt infection by getting a shot. And, just like that, I don't have to worry about smallpox pretty much ever. Because of science.

You can do much the same thing for your day by crafting a few personalized inoculations against the top-five critters that will fight against you enjoying these Oases.

The "Busy" Bacteria

Are you just too busy? People are continually in a state of perpetual motion. They work so hard, their minds constantly churning over all the work they need to do, that they find it hard to stop and take a break. I exposed this problem in my book *The Myth of Multitasking*, where I talk about how switching rapidly back and forth between tasks causes people to make more mistakes. People take longer to get things done, and their stress levels increase. Being busy intensifies multi-tasking, which is really just rapid switch-tasking in disguise. If you constantly condition yourself to be in a state of busy-ness, implementing the Culture of WIN can sometimes be a real shock to the system.

How do you inoculate yourself against that?

Build buffer time into your day. Buffer times are open spaces where you have scheduled time slots for potential attention switches.

Back in the '80s and '90s, traditional time management taught you to maximize the amount of work that you could do in the hours that you had, which at the time made sense. But back then, not every person in the world carried a magical, all-powerful rectangle in their pocket that they can use to summon any other person in the world in an instant. Back then, if we wanted to find out current stock prices, we had to call a broker . . . or wait until tomorrow when the *Wall Street*

Journal came out. If you wanted to switch programs on your Apple IIe, you had to turn it off, pull out the floppy disk, insert a new program, and then flip the power switch back on. It was about as productive as milking your own cow and then churning the resulting cream into butter.*

In the twenty-first century, we can interrupt others—or ourselves!—on a whim. Our challenge is not time management—it's focus management. We are constantly being bombarded by events that makes us switch our attention. They are inevitable. They are pervasive. And if we do not leave room in our schedule for these inevitable switches, we will be unprepared for them.

For every hour that you work, you want to create about ten minutes of free time. This means that many of my clients schedule fifty-minute meetings rather than ones lasting sixty minutes. Or you can do twenty-five-minute meetings instead of thirty minutes. You get the idea. The good news is that some programs, like Google Calendar, have a setting that you can switch on for "speedy meetings" that automatically put this in place.

If you get in the habit of leaving just a little bit of room, you'll not only be better prepared and less stressed out, but you'll also be in a position where you readily enjoy these Oases when the time comes.

• •

Protect yourself against being too busy by building buffer space into your schedule. Take a look at the next seven

---

*Yes, I exaggerate. But I earned the right. I lived through it.

days on your calendar. Make sure that for every hour you work, you have at least ten minutes of buffer time.

The "Guilty" Plague

You may recognize this tactic from the use of *deserve* in the Culture of WISH. Guilt will certainly not let go easily. If it already has a hold on you, you are going to be challenged with self-shaming thoughts.

Why should you enjoy a moment for this fun little Oasis when your team members, employees, or family members are still working? Why do you get this but they don't? It doesn't seem fair, does it? Who do you think you are?

Sound familiar?

Remember, this system we're setting up is not about deserving an Oasis. Deserving has nothing to do with it. This is about requiring a WIN. You need this to perform better. Oases don't get in the way of work—they make work better.

Plus, the people around you should be doing the same thing! They should be taking their scheduled Oases as well. You can both set an example and give them the gift of greater enjoyment and productivity by showing them that you know how to use your License to Have Fun. Think they need more convincing? If only there were a book you could give them. . . .

In all seriousness, though, the influence of those around you significantly impacts your own attitude about having fun. Talk to them about the importance of the change you've made and encourage them to do the same. Consider how much happier you would be and how much more work you could accomplish if you were taking your daily Oases and knew the people around you were doing the same.

Want to get inoculated from guilt? Get people to join the party.

· ·

Protect yourself against the plague of guilt by helping others buy into the power of having fun. Share some principles from this book with them, and encourage them to set their own Oases.

The "Meh" Virus

The third obstacle you may face is simply not being up for it. This issue is surprisingly common. Perhaps you've experienced the following: You're in the mode of working constantly. Your mindset is "go, go, go." Suddenly, the time arrives on your calendar to take a break and go for a walk—are you kidding me? No, I've been working on these reports. I'm on fire. Why should I stop midstream and go do something as silly as watch a Netflix show for thirty minutes?

One principle of success is to say no to distractions and interruptions. An equally powerful principle of success is to say yes to making time for yourself and your loved ones. You can't afford to be passive about having fun.

The virus of apathy requires a two-step inoculation. First, in addition to adding the buffer space that I mentioned before, schedule some transition time just before your Oases. Avoid parking mind-grabbing and body-intensive activities just before an Oasis. Rather, try to do these kinds of activities right after an Oasis. This way, you'll have an infusion of energy and tackle intense work with great focus.

Second, assign a value of some kind to the Oasis. In its simplest form, this means telling yourself how valuable this little walk, nap, or dance party is. Write it into the calendar that this is worth $100 per hour, your sanity, or having a better relationship with people around you.

Does this sound strange? Give it a try. By assigning a value, you're inoculating yourself against the idea that this Oasis is something you should do only if and when you feel up to it. For example, I mentioned that I enjoy a little video game time. The value of that Oasis is connected to my ability to focus on my family. My children come into my home office at 5:00 p.m. and tell me it's time to go downstairs. If I haven't taken that Oasis of blasting a few zombies, then, when I go downstairs, it's me who's now the zombie . . . still so focused on work that I'm oblivious to the needs and attention of my wife and children. Staring into space.

When it happens, my wife—who hates video games—wisely asks, "Did you play video games?"

I sheepishly reply, "No."

Her reply: "What's wrong with you?"

She recognizes the value of this Oasis in my life because of the impact it has on her life. You can create that same kind of value association in your mind.

Protect yourself against apathy by scheduling some transition time before each Oasis on your calendar. Also, consider adding a statement of value to each scheduled Oasis,

such as, "This is worth it because it will help me be a better friend."

The "Difficulty" Disease

This issue often challenges the larger monthly or yearly Oases.

Aren't major vacations just a pain? Isn't finding a way to get some time off work just a tremendous hassle? Gotta find someone to fill in for you, gotta find someone to watch the kids, gotta . . . you name it. Why should having fun be so much work? Right?

I had a client who once jokingly said to me that he should take a vacation every week because he's always more productive just before and after. He'd be in a hurry to get everything done just before he left, and then he would have to catch up and do everything after returning. While there's a hint of truth to that sentiment, that's actually the opposite of what the inoculation is all about.

You can minimize the level of difficulty by giving yourself prescheduled catch-up time both before and after that major Oasis. You're going to need several extra hours, if not a full day, on either side of that Oasis. Take several hours just before to clear out your inboxes and several hours just after to do the same. Veterans of my Time Management Fundamentals course on LinkedIn Learning will recognize this time as "processing."

In one sentence: Processing is the act of taking everything that you have in your email and physical inboxes and deciding what, when, and where.

My clients do this with each and every item until they reach an empty inbox. Most people can get this done in an average of five hours a week. This means that if you're going to be unavailable for work for one week while you're off on a big Oasis, you're going to want to schedule five hours of processing both before you leave and after you get back.

Spend extra time processing before you go on a vacation, and you'll leave for Disney World with the ability to enjoy yourself, knowing you didn't leave anything undone. And when you return from the Oasis, your prescheduled processing time will give you confidence that you can start the new week up to date and ready to move forward.

Protect yourself against the "difficulty" disease by scheduling processing time before and after major Oases. Look ahead on your calendar and find your next yearly Oasis. Make sure you have extra processing time before and after if you will be away for several days.

The "Cost" Cold

When I start talking about the concept of an Oasis, people get these grand ideas of going on vacations and visiting exotic locations or immediately spending money on a new ninety-inch, uber-mega-HD-smart-TV and reclining sectional couches. If that's the idea that you've gotten from this book, we need to pause and take a breath. Most everything that you've put on the Oasis List should be affordable and require little time.

The eighteenth-century poet Alexander Pope once penned,

"Blessed is the man who expects nothing, for he shall never be disappointed."

Let's make an alteration to turn this into an Oasis-based maxim: "Blessed is the man who *sets affordable expectations*, for he shall never be disappointed."

Begin well within your budget. If, right now, you can afford only $10 on an Oasis, then spend $5. If you want an Oasis that's going to cost $1,000, but that little voice in the back of your head—which sounds strangely like Dave Ramsey—tells you you're over budget, then slow down. Stay well below what you can afford. Remember: Oases can and should be inexpensive.

If you have a substantial yearly Oasis that will require more money than you've spent in the past, begin budgeting today. Many banks will allow you to set up a second subaccount online. Name it "Oasis Account," and set up automatic monthly withdrawals if possible. That way you don't have to think about it. Over time, you can increase your budget gradually as your value per hour increases.

Protect yourself against the "cost" cold by evaluating your Oases and making sure they are well below your available budget. If you have a yearly Oasis that will require more money, set up a special account to begin saving for it.

Of course, there may be other sneaky sicknesses that creep into your life, trying to prevent you from enjoying your much-needed Oases. When they arise, ask yourself, "What is needed to protect my Oasis time?" The most successful people I know are sensitive to obstacles. The moment they see them, they work on finding a solution. Do the same.

If you run into an obstacle I haven't covered here, feel free to reach out to me at **DaveCrenshaw.com/ask**. I'll be glad to help you find a solution.

CHAPTER 9

Stage Five: Enjoying Your Oases

From a psychological standpoint, I find the enjoyment part of an Oasis most fascinating. Why? Because many people just plain don't *feel* it.

Feel what? Happiness, joy, elation—that whatever they're doing is pleasurable. There is a shocking epidemic of emotional numbness, especially when it comes to enjoying the simplest pleasures in life.

In candid, private conversations that I have with my coaching clients, I find more and more people wondering whether they are able to feel emotions at all. I even had a client wonder out loud whether he was a sociopath. He isn't, in case you're wondering. But because he felt so numb, to him, it felt like a legitimate question.

Why do so many of us feel that we're not connecting emotionally to what is happening around us? Some people face a psychological smattering of unique challenges; I'll mention mine later in this chapter.

However, in my experience of working with executives around the world, I find most of us feel this way as the result of cultural conditioning. Our world is in constant motion, with us continually jumping back and forth between email and the phone. We are perpetually connected online. The news is hardwired to promote that which grabs attention, and negative always outsells the positive in that department. We are increasingly looking for a payout via the social-media, peer-approval vending machine. FoMO, or the fear of missing out, has become a primary motivator in so many lives.

The Culture of WISH feeds this frenzied attitude by constantly whipping us from behind. Work faster! Work harder! Keep up with your neighbors! You're not good enough. Someday, maybe, you will be. But certainly not now. Get to work!

And, in the hurricane of all these distractions, we forget to pay attention to our emotions . . . especially the positive ones.

Let's view this problem as we would physical training. Our ability to feel and enjoy is a muscle. It's a mental, emotional muscle that we must strengthen. The more we strengthen it, the easier it will be to feel joy in simple moments.

This mindset doesn't come from an outsider looking in or from some individual who's been perfect and helped others to become perfect. To the contrary, my past and present include an unsavory genetic cocktail of mental-health challenges. Please forgive this momentary detour into my psyche. I'm not telling you this in the spirit of making this all about me. It's more the idea of, "Oh my gosh, if a messed-up dude like Dave can do this, I most certainly can!"

Despite being a guy who regularly travels the world, meeting new and exciting people and getting up in front of large audiences, I feel socially inept. To me, social gatherings are mystifying and painful. As comedian Brian Regan said, "Parties aren't set up like [a comedy show]. I don't show up at parties and people go, 'All right, we'll all get over here, and you get over there.'"

This feeling—or lack thereof—is the result of a lot of influences, both biological and familial. I grew up learning to second-guess myself constantly. I was never certain whether my emotions were valid, an overreaction, an underreaction, or just plain me being weird.

There was a time in my life when one of my children would hug me, and I'd feel nothing. No emotional response. No sense of joy. Just a blank expression. That was a difficult thing to reconcile as someone who deeply believes that my wife and children should be some of the greatest sources of joy in my life.

Life is much better now, thanks to a little system I developed to reboot my personal, emotional computer. It has also helped many people I've worked with in a private coaching context. Put this process into practice, and you can feel amazing and enjoy those Oases and be more aware of the good things that are happening to you.

Meaningful enjoyment promotes success. Simplifying science greatly, the natural chemicals swirling around in your brain play a huge role in your enjoyment. As we discussed in chapter 5 on permission, dopamine—among other chemicals—plays a critical role in your success. Yet, when we fail to experience *any* kind of emotion, we're stonewalling our own success. No enjoyment, no future motivation.

Time to break down that wall. There are three steps to help you enjoy your Oases:

1. Mentally acknowledge
2. Emotionally acknowledge
3. Verbally acknowledge

Mentally Acknowledge

For a moment, try to remember the last good, positive thing that happened to you.

What comes to mind? Anything? If you struggle to remember something, it's likely you were moving so quickly that the moment passed by like a billboard on the freeway, with you flying by at seventy miles an hour. You saw it, but it didn't register.

The cure? Whenever something happens, simply take a moment to tag it mentally.

Let's practice using that positive memory I just asked you to recall. Even if you have to go back a few weeks to remember something, hold that moment in your mind for a bit.

Mentally acknowledging means that you take moments and simply think to yourself, "That was enjoyable . . ." or "That was fun . . ."

For example:

"That was enjoyable just to go for a walk in the fresh air."

"That was fun to crank up that music and dance like a mad fool."

"That was fun to go for a ride around the canyon with my window rolled down."

"That was enjoyable to get to know a complete stranger."

Consider the alternative. How many times have you failed to acknowledge good moments because you were multitasking or just being busy? I occasionally catch myself doing this when work takes me to speak in a country or city I've never visited before. After a long flight, the temptation is just to plop into the back of a taxi, pull out my phone, and rifle through emails. Yet outside, a whole new experience of sights, sounds, and faces is passing me by. Knowing that I have this weakness, I force myself to look out the window, soak it in, and simply tell myself, "That's cool."

Sometimes, we block out positive moments because we've conditioned our minds to continually be on the move, poking holes in our current joy.

For example, I asked a CEO client of mine to tell me about something positive that happened in the last year. She started talking about a huge client who had brought in amazing revenue . . . but couldn't stop there. She continued about how that was scary because her company maybe, perhaps, possibly wasn't diversified enough, and so they were at risk. She was skilled at taking a positive and spinning it into a negative.

If that's something you do, I'll tell you the same thing I told her: Stop. Go back and just let the good and happy moment sit for ten seconds. No need to connect it to something negative. Yes, there's power in planning, but let's not allow our concern for the future get in the way of our enjoyment of the moment. Enjoy it. Then, later, return to the concern you have and work on finding a solution.

For now, tell that big brain of yours that a positive moment just occurred, so pay attention! Help your brain pause and strengthen the neural pathways that recognize when something wonderful is occurring.

Emotionally Acknowledge

After mentally acknowledging a fun moment, the next step is to acknowledge it emotionally. The simplest way to do this is via a question such as, "How did that make me feel?" Then, take a moment to respond to it.

"How did it make me feel to go for that brief jog around the block?"

"How did it make me feel to water the radishes in my garden?"

"How did it make me feel to take a break and play video games for a bit?"

"How did it make me feel to enjoy a tasty beverage?"

This type of question helps your mind transition from the intellectual side—just paying attention—to the emotional body chemistry that's occurring in the moment. When good things happen, good stuff is going on inside your body. You're built that way: to produce positive chemical reactions internally when something positive happens to you. The more you take the time to assess it, the more aware you become of what your body is doing.

And the more aware you become of the good feelings you're experiencing, the more you'll want to have those feelings occur in the future. What we focus on becomes more meaningful and repeatable.

Verbally Acknowledge

The final step, after mentally and emotionally acknowledging an enjoyable moment, is to acknowledge it verbally.

The moment you say something out loud, it adds the additional sensory impact of both doing something and hearing it. This action further strengthens the value of that moment in your brain, building your emotional muscles even more.

Now, of course, you may want to be judicious about how loud you say it or the moments at which you say it. If a whole company had this book, it would be strange if everyone walked around saying, "That was great!" to themselves all day. I could see customers being weirded out by that kind of behavior.

This principle is flexible. Find a way to express the moment in a way that matches who you are.

You can do it quietly. You can whisper it to yourself. You can record a voice message to yourself. The power of hearing it in your own voice will further strengthen your ability to enjoy amazing, happy occurrences in the future. Some people also find that expressing thanks through prayer is a meaningful way to do this. Or you can simply tell a friend, "That was awesome."

Not comfortable with saying something out loud? Then let your fingers do the talking. You can start a journal to record these moments; perhaps call it the *Oasis Journal*. Just keep it simple and short. No need to write a detailed Victorian novel every time you go bird-watching. Designate a section in a notetaking app, such as Evernote or OneNote, or on the back of a little notepad. When you experience a little Oasis, simply write it down.

Dear Diary,
Today, I listened to music. It made me feel happy and relaxed. Life's good!

Easy peasy.

Brain. Heart. Mouth.

By strengthening the power of these Oases in your brain, you increase the value of them. You will begin to recognize them as moments that give you strength and power.

Since you obviously won't want to reread this section to remember what you're supposed to do when something positive happens, here's a simple trick to remember:

Brain. Heart. Mouth.

Brain: mentally acknowledge by thinking, "That was fun . . ."

Heart: emotionally acknowledge by asking, "How did it make me feel?"

Mouth: verbally acknowledge by saying, "That was good!"

Brain. Hearth. Mouth. You may want to touch them as you do them . . . like head, shoulders, knees, and toes.

Follow this pattern whenever you experience something that's just a little bit enjoyable, and you will begin to notice more and more fun and enjoyable moments happening all around you.

Putting It into Action

Before we finish this chapter, I want to take a moment to practice this right now. There is power both in repetition and in doing something that relates to what you just read. Consider for a moment, what was the last positive thing that happened to you? What's the first thing that comes to mind?

. . . .

Write down one fun moment that happened to you in the last day or week.

_____

Brain. Acknowledge it mentally by thinking, "That was a great moment."

Heart. Emotionally assess how it felt by asking, "How did that make me feel?"

Mouth. Finally, say it out loud. If you're in a crowded place, you'll still get points if you prefer to mumble it. Extra mega-bonus points if you shout it out in a restaurant! Just kidding, don't do that . . . at least not with this book in your hand.

Wrapping Up the Personal Oasis

By following these five stages of the Personal Oasis, you're now establishing a powerful habit in your life. It's not a habit of doing hard, painful things. It's the habit of doing pleasant, fun things. Of enjoying life more.

This simple little habit of WINing every day will yield massive results in your life as you continue to do it. Enjoying an Oasis once is not enough. The power is in the compounded strength of daily Oasis after daily Oasis. Of weekly Oasis building upon weekly Oasis. Of wonderful and happy moments happening each month and celebrating bigger Oases every year.

As you experience the power of having fun, I'd love to hear your story. Pictures would be especially appreciated if you want to send them. Please share your experiences with me by sending an email to **fun@DaveCrenshaw.com**, or share it on social media with the hashtag, #PowerofHavingFun. I'll be looking for you!

Now, let's move on to creating Oases for the people that you love the most.

Part Three

The Family Oasis

CHAPTER 10

Stage One: Family Permission

While we've discussed finding little nuggets of joy in your personal life, we've yet to discover that balance for the people in your family. Having fun with your family has five stages, just as your Personal Oases do. Yet how you apply this process to your family is a bit different.

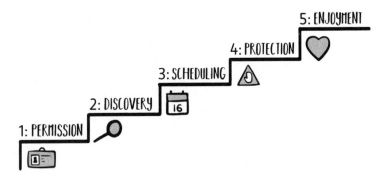

Remember, when I say *family,* I mean the most flexible definition possible. For the sake of clarity, family can include your traditional family—if you're close to them—as well as best friends, parents, siblings, boyfriends/girlfriends, the grandparents you never forget to visit on weekends, your party-animal roommates, and even your trusted dog Sparky.*

Let's get right down to it. If these people care about you, they want to see you and spend time with you. Being with you is a strength to them and vice versa. You must make time for these people. Not just for you. Not just for your work. But for them. Yes, you're doing work to make money, which is important for taking care of necessities—for you and those that you love. Yet, after you've satisfied the physiological rung in Maslow's proverbial hierarchy of needs, what they really want is you.

Remember that survey of children around the country? The one where we asked kids about having fun? They had some interesting insights to offer about family, too.

One ten-year-old boy in Arizona stated, "Money is important, but for a kid, it's more important the time parents spend with their kids. I prefer to go to the park with my family than an expensive gift or a video game."

How about this eight-year-old girl in New York: "My mommy always works, and I always tell her to come and play games with me. I love when we dance together."

Then there's the ten-year-old girl in Michigan who couldn't have been clearer when she suggested, "Kids really want more time with [their parents], more than toys and new stuff."

The time that we spend with family can't wait until tomorrow. The Culture of WIN is about making it worth it now.

---

*Your distant, hippie, thrice-removed cousin, who waits tables and surfs on a beach in Argentina, doesn't count.

The good news is that, like scheduling our personal wins, making a change to have more fun is, well, fun!

Finding Family Permission

Your first step toward giving yourself permission to enjoy Family Oases begins with a simple question:

• •

Please write your answer to this question: Why is it important for me to spend time with my family?

_____

_____

_____

Candidly, I find a whole lot of people struggle in this department. Maybe we don't have a relationship that we consider positive. Maybe we are afraid of being vulnerable. We feel our imperfections hurt the people around us. Maybe, just maybe, we are caught up in WISHing our problems away: it's not great now, but someday, hopefully, these relationships will improve.

Part of the goal of this chapter is to give you the warm fuzzies—the real kind. These positive thoughts will form reasons to either strengthen your resolve and build up relationships into something glorious or provide you with the motivation to restart.

Right now, wherever you're at in this process emotionally, just trust me for now. Having fun with people you care about has the life- and career-boosting potential of a hundred ter-awatts of power.

Let's explore why Family Oases are both necessary and powerful.

Reason One: Relationships Can Always Be Strengthened

In my work with leaders, I often straddle the line between business coach and personal therapist. Occasionally, clients tell me secrets that they haven't told their spouse. Often, they tell me that their marriages no longer have the connection they once had. I can't tell you how often I've heard others lamenting, "We're drifting apart."

The natural question to ask a person experiencing this malaise is, "Are you spending time together?" It's a simple thing, just being in each other's presence. Yet for some reason, this is difficult for people invested in their careers, especially when spouses work together.

According to a report from the National Marriage Project, married people who had "couple time" or a "date night" at least once per week were about 3.5 times more likely to report having "very happy" marriages compared with those who spent less time together.

Additionally, if couples spent at least one dedicated time together per week, they reported higher satisfaction in communication and sexually—both spouses were more than three times more likely to report higher satisfaction in the bedroom.

And this need not be just about marriage. The simple action of having consistent fun time together can do wonders for any relationship.

Reason Two: Some Things Happen Only Once, So Stay in the Moment

Life throws you curveballs sometimes. More often than not, they are little surprises that charm you. You sit back and enjoy those moments.

Unless you're buried head down in the glowing screen of the Culture of WISH.

You might say, "Walking Sparky isn't a priority right now because there's stuff that needs to be done. Later, I'll have more time for a walk." Right?

Or, if you have a boyfriend, "It's okay if I skip date night because if I cruise through these expense reports, we'll have plenty of time for dates some other time." Right?

Or, if you're a parent, "It's okay if I don't show up for my daughter's soccer game because she'll have another one next week." Right?

Don't worry. You can always make up for lost time, right?

Time is a flowing river, and it is foolish to think that you can paddle back upstream. Your child is going to take his or her first step only once. Your significant other will be in desperate need of a listening ear for that particular problem only once. You get only one chance to go to your sister's wedding . . . well, knowing your sister, maybe not. You get the idea.

All of us have missed these moments. Even with the best of intentions, we cannot be omnipresent, nor are we perfect. However, there is a huge difference between missing moments because we're human and missing moments because we failed to make an effort.

Bronnie Ware was a hospice nurse who worked with end-of-life patients. She wrote a book and was interviewed many times about the "top five regrets of the dying." She would ask her patients about their greatest regrets. One of the most common regrets, in addition to wishing that they hadn't worked as hard, was wishing that they had had the courage to express their feelings as well as to stay in touch with their friends.

Sometime in the future, you too will reach the end of your days. By living a life full of Family Oases, these kinds of regrets need not be yours.

Reason Three: Having Fun with Family Increases Your Success at Work

You read that right.

Your family can become a source of strength for your career. It's quite simple: when you feel closer to loved ones, you'll also perform better at work.

On the surface, it makes sense, right? The more emotionally built up we are at home, the stronger we'll feel at work. It's something we rarely discuss let alone acknowledge on an intellectual level. Yet we've all seen the impact of the reverse. How many times at the office have you seen the guy with a five o'clock shadow and the distinct look of having slept on the couch the night before?

This is referred to as the "work-home resources model" in a study by Lieke ten Brummelhuis and Arnold Bakker, published by the American Psychological Association. They found that spouses who have a good and stable marriage are more likely to experience better performance at work.

Again, I've seen that positive effect come from other relationships in the lives of my clients. When they have been able to get closer to their children and other loved ones, their confidence increases and success flows more easily to them. Want to boost your career? Make spending time with family a priority.

And, here's a bonus benefit: the time you spend with them will boost their performance at work, too! It makes sense, right? Since these Oases are a party for two or more, the benefits flow in all directions. So, want your loved ones to succeed? Have fun with them.

Reason Four: You're Building Something That Lasts Far beyond Work

What we create with our family has the potential to last not just for a lifetime but for generations.

Occasionally, I'll attend a family reunion with my in-laws. It's somewhat overwhelming. My wife and I have established that I have some issues when it comes to unstructured mingling with large groups of humans. And, boy oh boy, is a reunion of my in-laws a large group.

My wife's grandparents began a remarkable yet humble relationship as a farmer and his wife in northern Utah, when they married in 1941. They had five boys, who had thirty children in total. This led to 117 great-grandchildren and counting, and—as of this writing—three great-great-grandchildren . . . and counting. In short, their marriage has left its mark on more than 150 people.

That's not old-fashioned, that's just life.

If you're not a mother or father, you can influence the lives of others by making a concerted effort to spend time with them. There are plenty of examples of individuals who have left their mark on many people without having had children or gotten married.

You don't need to have the traditional nuclear family to have a lasting impact on those whom you've labeled as "family." The choice you make to spend time with them on a consistent basis can send ripples that will last for centuries.

Reason Five: You're Creating Lasting, Positive Memories

When you engage in these Family Oases, you're building up a deep reservoir of positive memories for both you and those you love. This deepens and strengthens your relationship.

Consider someone whom you personally love and admire. Now consider the memories you have of this person. What stands out to you? Unless you are a savant, odds are you don't remember every single moment of every day. Instead, you're likely to remember just a handful of sweet moments—moments largely out of the ordinary.

Our brain, for a variety of reasons, is wired that way. We're attuned to registering things that are out of the norm. By taking time to create Oases with your family, you're creating a kind of memory bond from your loved ones to you and vice versa.

Remember that Oasis journal I mentioned earlier in the book? Think of this as your memory reserve; a magic treasure chest that you can turn to when you're feeling gloomy, down in the dumps, or just plain bummed. You can read your journal for a quick, feel-good dopamine rush with zero side effects.

Reason Six: You're Rewarding Your Family

Face the facts: you are magnificent.

You may not think it. You're skeptical when you hear it. You may or may not love hearing it said. Yet it's true.

Just being around you lifts others up and makes them feel incredible. Is that part of your brain that loves positive attention humming? Good.

Give people the opportunity to bask in your glorious presence. Too often, in a reasonable attempt to #stayhumble, we forget how much of an influence we are on people. Creating

Oases gives you an opportunity to be a positive influence on your family.

There are roles that come with the territory of influencing children: teacher, nurturer, provider, protector, therapist. The list of titles is substantial; just don't forget about *numero uno*: hero.

So, go on. Put on your cape. Be their hero.

My wife and I experience this weekly, if not daily, with our young 'uns. My wife will leave to run a short errand in the neighborhood. As soon as she gets back and the garage door closes, the kids jump up and scream, "Mommy!" and greet her with a hug. Now imagine me, sitting on the couch incredulously with a "What am I? Chopped liver?" face. Of course, I'm mostly kidding. I too get my fair share of rock-star treatment from the kids just for showing up and being Dad.

Everyone can. You can be somebody's hero.

Do you have a picture of why these family wins aren't just a good idea but rather a necessity? Do you feel the motivation and, more importantly, the permission to set a schedule for spending time with loved ones? That was the goal in this chapter.

Once again, I hand you the permit you need to move forward with having family fun. The license is yours. Drive joyously.

If you didn't do so in the Personal Oasis section, turn to the back of the book where there's a handy-dandy, premade license for you. You can fill it out with your name and picture and add a motivational quote to remind you of the importance of enjoying these Family Oases. Here's an example:

"We are fa-mi-ly. I got all my sisters with me."

Now let's figure out how best to spend time with those special people that get to spend time with you.

CHAPTER 11

Stage Two: Discovering Family Fun

On one occasion, I found myself speaking in a special location: Tanzania, in the city of Dar es Salaam. One might be tempted to refer to this place as an actual oasis. There was something surreal about working a room and speaking as the waves crashed along the shore of Coco Beach, with the ocean breeze wafting into the room.

My seminar to local business leaders covered what we've been discussing: taking more time with family members and enjoying these moments with the people we love. The day after the event, I managed to get some feedback from a few of the attendees. One story stayed with me.

Apparently, one attendee went back home to his wife and told her something along the lines of "This guy from America had a great idea. He said we should schedule daily, weekly, and monthly time for just you and me. What do you want to do?"

After she got over the initial shock, the man's wife didn't need more than a second to think about it. She replied, "Once a month, let's sleep under the stars."

When I tell this story at an event, half the audience usually projects an audible "Awww." The other half? A soft groan.

The point? A Family Oasis isn't about you and what you want. You've already scheduled your *me* time with the Personal Oasis. Now, it's *us* time. It's *them* time.

This isn't to imply that you won't get a say in the matter. Just keep in mind that the Family Oasis is primarily about your family's wishes.

Brainstorming the Family Oasis

Let's start by imagining this process with your significant other, whether that's a spouse, boyfriend/girlfriend, or fiancé. You get the idea. Don't have a significant other? Pick your dearest friend.

The first step is to set aside time to talk comfortably about a Family Oasis. Schedule this to happen in a place where both of you can enjoy the conversation, relax, have plenty of time, and speak candidly with each other. An hour should do the trick.

Oh, and set this up *now*.

Contact your significant other to set up a time when you can plan some Oases together. Schedule time in both of your calendars for about an hour.

Did you do it? Good work! But you're not done yet!

I've provided you with a worksheet to help make this a little bit easier. Flip over to the next page for a second. Look familiar? This worksheet is set up similarly to your Personal Oasis worksheet, with one dramatic difference. The question that you want to ask people is, "If we spent time together, what would be meaningful to you?"

In the first column, you'll want to work with your loved ones to create a raw list of ideas. What activities would be meaningful to them? At first, this is just brainstorming. Create a long running list of all the ideas that you can come up with. You may be surprised how often what your loved one suggests is simple and very doable.

I'll never forget a conversation I had with one leader. He told me that he didn't think his wife was happy about how much time he spent at work. I set up a conference call on the spot with all three of us and asked what she wanted from her husband every day.

She responded, "Be home at 5:30 every day."

Yeah, sometimes it's as simple as that! Don't be shocked if what your loved one wants to do is just bask in your glorious presence.

Another client told me it was meaningful to his wife for him to cook a family meal once or twice a week. That became a nice weekly Oasis for them. You get the idea.

• •

During your scheduled time, brainstorm a list of possible Family Oasis activities by asking your significant other, "What, to you, would be a meaningful activity for us to do together?"

What would be meaningful to them?	Why would it be meaningful?

After completing your initial brainstorm, move on the second column:

• •

After brainstorming a list of ideas with your loved one, ask, "Why is this activity meaningful to you?"

This is critical because it will help you discover the thought process, logic, and emotion behind why your loved one is listing this activity. Knowing this will increase your motivation, and it will help your loved one feel validated because you took the time to understand them better.

Done with that step? Now it's time to transfer this info onto a more detailed worksheet that closely matches what we did for your Personal Oasis.

You'll see several columns: "Under 15 minutes" for daily Family Oases, "15 to 90 minutes" for either daily or weekly Oases, "90 minutes to 12 hours" for weekly or monthly Oases, "one half-day to three days" for monthly or yearly Oases, and "More than 3 days" for the yearly flavor of Family Oases.

Length (Category)	Activities	Estimated cost
(Example) Under 15 minutes (daily)	*Sit on the porch in the eveing and enjoy talking with each other for a bit*	*Zero*
Under 15 minutes (daily)		
15 to 90 minutes (daily or weekly)		
90 minutes to 12 hours (weekly or monthly)		
One half-day to 3 days (monthly or yearly)		
More than 3 days (yearly)		

Use the list you created in the Family Oasis brainstorming exercise, and transfer each activity that you would enjoy onto the worksheet above. Categorize each idea according to the amount of time it would require. Then make a note about the estimated cost next to each activity.

Congratulations, you now have a start on the Family Oasis list for one VIP in your life!

Expanding the List

Now, what about your children or other family members? Well, it's the same kind of discussion. However, I recommend that it be just a touch more casual. After all, I don't think Grandma wants to go to a romantic restaurant and eat chocolate-covered strawberries with you.

For example, approach a buddy with, "Sup dude? I've been thinking we should start hanging out more. Let's set up a schedule for us to kick back and eat pizza together. My treat, bro!"

You don't have to sound like a snowboarder from 1997. Make it your own. Just be sure to make it about the other person.

You may want to enter these conversations with an idea of the frequency of Oases you want to have. For example, while I recommend having daily, weekly, monthly, and yearly Oases with a significant other, I don't believe it's realistic or necessary to have a daily Oasis for every one of your friends or every member of your family circle.

I have three children, and even though I love them, I can't operate like Bob Saget's Danny Tanner from *Full House*. I don't think it's necessary to take time out of every day for each of my precious little nuggets to have a scheduled warm and fuzzy moment individually.*

What I can do is a monthly Oasis with each of them individually. I can set aside a certain weekend every single month for one of them and then create a pattern of allowing them to choose what we are going to do that day. My youngest will be four at the release of this book. She and I can have a special midday lunch after preschool. I told her that I scheduled this time with her, and she said, "You're the best daddy in the whole world!" So it must be true.

With your friends, it's likely not going to be a daily Oasis. Perhaps once a week you go on a little shopping excursion or tailgate with bratwursts at the stadium. Or maybe you have some college friends that have since gone in separate directions. This might be a great opportunity for an annual trip. I have a coaching client on the East Coast who does this. He calls it his "Fandango" trip, after the classic movie.

That part is up to you. You can also choose how to discuss this with your friends. Just have an understanding up front of what you are willing to do and what is not practical. Just as you did with your spouse or significant other, brainstorm and discuss what would be meaningful to you.

Be open to everything. A friend once told me a story about his four-year-old son. The two spent time together weekly. One day, he asked his son what he wanted to do most, and his son said, "I want to go to the mall and ride the escalators."

Talk about the little things! To the credit of this open-minded father, he and his son went to the mall and treated

---

*After all, I have my buddy John Stamos to worry about, too.

the escalator like the Kingda Ka roller coaster, as people walked in and out of Delia's and Hot Topic.

Take a moment and decide when you can connect with another family member to brainstorm some Oasis ideas. Then schedule that time in both of your calendars.

Now that you have some fun activities figured out for your Family Oasis, it's time we move on to the next stage of adding them to your mutual schedules.

CHAPTER 12

Stage Three: Scheduling Family Oases

This is a moment of commitment. Are you ready?

Let's schedule your Family Oases.

We want to set up these Family Oases to happen at a time that works easily for both you and the other family members involved. Also, we'll want to allow for extra room in your schedule so that you don't feel rushed. This shouldn't feel like a chore to be checked off your to-do list. After all, what good is an Oasis if it is only a mirage?

Let's begin with the easiest possible thing that you can schedule: the daily Family Oasis with your significant other.

· ·

Find a time to chat with your closest loved one. In the conversation, schedule a brief, recurring daily Family Oasis for the two of you to enjoy together.

It's likely that you'll experience what many of my clients have reported—that this act of setting up time for an Oasis brought them closer to their loved one . . . even before they did anything!

Scheduling the Weekly Family Oasis

Let's move on to the next step and create a weekly win. Remember, if you have a weekly Oasis, like watching Monday night *WWE Raw* (I won't judge), you don't need to have a daily Oasis on Mondays. Let's not double-dip the chip!

Incidentally, if you have a significant other, when it comes to the weekly Oasis, I strongly suggest that you schedule a date night. The activities in those date nights can change, but the consistency is critical. For most people, a weekend night will work well for this, but don't be afraid to be creative.

One client, a New York executive, has a weekly Friday morning breakfast with his wife. My wife and I have Saturday afternoon dates to avoid evening crowds. Any time or day of the week is fair game.

During your conversation, also schedule a recurring weekly Family Oasis for both of you to enjoy together.

At this point in the process, you should have two new appointments on both of your calendars. You should have a daily recurring Oasis and a weekly recurring Oasis with at least one family member. Remember, this is in addition to your Personal Oasis. Time for them; time for you. Got it? That's the real kind of balance that we're trying to create in your life.

Scheduling the Monthly Family Oasis

Now it's time to move on to the more substantial monthly Family Oasis. This is going to take more coordination and planning. Occasionally, you may have to be flexible with how this is established. For the monthly Oasis, you'll want to scan through the Family Oasis worksheet under the half-day to three-day activities. Think three-day weekend or an extended afternoon at a beach or park on the weekend with your family. Then try to find a pattern that you can establish as recurring.

Imagine you want to have a monthly Family Oasis at a park. A consistent pattern could be something like the third Sunday of every month. This allows the pattern to continue independently of the changing dates within a month. It also avoids many of the conflicts that might occur during a typical work week.

Occasionally, you may want to use the traditional* three-day weekend to establish this. Just be cautious, as these don't occur every single month. If you choose to use holiday weekends, create a reminder for yourself to check in advance for three-day weekends each month.

---

*At least in the United States.

Schedule time with a family member to discuss creating a recurring monthly Family Oasis to enjoy together.

Scheduling the Yearly Family Oasis

Now for the big one: the yearly Family Oasis. Usually, this is going to be something like a family vacation. However, I've seen some clients vary this from year to year. For instance, one year they go on a vacation, but the following year they make a substantial—yet affordable—purchase that everyone can use, such as a swing set or ping-pong table.

The same primary rule for your budget that we had for the Personal Oases applies to the family variety: stay well within your means. By this I mean 50 percent or less of what you think you can afford. It does you and your family little good if you break the bank for a big Family Oasis and then feel stressed out the rest of the year because of financial issues.

All of these considerations take some regular planning. Don't rush it. You can even look nine to eleven months out. What we're trying to do is create a solid commitment well in advance by blocking out specific dates for your Family Oasis. This reminds you to not schedule other activities during that time, and to let others know you'll be unavailable.

• •

Take a moment to scan the next twelve months of your schedule. When would it make sense to make this yearly Family Oasis happen? Set up a conversation to discuss options with family members and commit to a date.

You'll also want to consider when to start planning. However much time is appropriate, create a reminder for yourself to have a conversation with your family about how you're all going to make this Oasis happen.

All too often, I see people not taking a vacation simply because they're too busy to plan one. On the flip side, I've seen clients who are so caught up in work they believe vacation time is the only time they have to plan their *next* vacation.

A CEO once told me that she was lounging on a beach in a beautiful tropical location—the white sand under her feet, the sound of the waves, a tropical drink melting in her hand. Yet, instead of soaking in paradise, she kept scrolling through her phone, planning her next vacation. When she caught herself doing this, she exclaimed, "Holy crap. I have a disease!"

Many of us have the same disease, but we can break this pattern by scheduling time to plan for Family Oases. That way, we give ourselves permission to enjoy the sights, sounds, sand, and surf when it's vacation time. Later, when it's appropriate, we can plan our next Oasis. Enjoyment must come first.

Also, you want to ensure that the Family Oasis becomes a yearly recurring event. Reviewing your yearly Oasis about two or three weeks after the fact is about right because it gives you time to enjoy and recover from it.

Schedule a reminder to review both your monthly and yearly Family Oases. For best results, schedule this reminder about two weeks after the yearly Family Oasis is set to occur.

During this follow-up planning, you might want to sit down with your family members and ask, "What did we like about that? What do we want to change? What do we want to do differently next time? Do we want to adjust the budget? Do we want to make the Oasis longer?" Your mind is still fresh about what was enjoyable (relaxing and watching the sunset) and what wasn't (waiting in line for two hours for that one ride that made you want to toss your cookies—no thank you!).

Once you get into a rhythm of establishing this first round of Family Oases, you can begin to be a little bit more flexible. Later, you can take a look at the other ideas you came up with when brainstorming with your family. You can also consider other family members you haven't created a plan with yet.

For now, the most important thing is to start somewhere—anywhere. Once you set these Oases up, be consistent with the schedule. Your family wants to know that they can depend on you to have a fun time.

Which is why it's now time to talk about protecting those Oases, especially when it comes to your family members!

CHAPTER 13

Stage Four: Protecting Family Oases

When it comes to protecting the Family Oasis, many of the same tactics we used to protect the Personal Oasis still apply. If you want an in-depth review, you may want to reread chapter 10. However, here is a quick recap to jog your memory:

1. Not enough time? Schedule buffer time in your day for when your schedule gets hectic.

2. Feeling guilty? Encourage others to schedule Oases, and remember that performance depends on these Oases!

3. Not feeling up to it? Leave free "buffer" time before, psych yourself up by remembering the value, and just do it!

4. Difficult vacation hassles? Book your trip in advance and establish time both before and after the vacation to get caught up on everything.

5. Too costly? Establish a budget, limited to 50 percent of what you can afford, and set up a savings account for the bigger monthly and yearly Oases.

You can apply these same tools to protect your Family Oases. There are also a couple of unique issues when it comes to having fun with loved ones. See if you've run into these obstacles before:

"We just don't feel close to each other."

Setting up time with loved ones is a great idea, but what if you're not feeling that close to a family member? There may be people that you love but, at the moment, you're just not comfortable around them. Perhaps you feel like they don't want to spend time with you or vice versa. What do you do then?

It makes sense. Relationships evolve. There are rough patches. Life is unpredictable.

Sometimes we just don't feel in sync with others. This is especially true in marriage. When we make the pledge to love someone "until death do us part," there isn't a clause for "assuming we don't kill each other first." Does your loved one prefer the toilet paper to hang over rather than under? Well, you're on your own for that one.

However, for more serious, ongoing issues, I'd recommend enlisting the services of a trusted therapist. These are people who can help you get closer to each other, especially in times of need. I have benefited from this. My wife has benefited from this. The clients that I coach have often improved their marriages by additionally enlisting the help of a therapist.

Bigger issues aside, all relationships are prone to drift due to atrophy. Think of your relationship like a plant. You need to nurture plants, right? My wife is amazing at many things— but a dedicated horticulturist she is not. She's a serial plant killer. She forgets to water and feed them. Pretty soon, our house begins to look like the last scene in a horror movie.

She's the fern equivalent of Hannibal Lecter . . . only these plants aren't edible.

Thankfully, she's not that way with our relationship.

If you want to have a close relationship with someone, you need to water it and feed it and spend time with it. You can help it grow simply by giving it more attention. Crafting that Family Oasis and regularly spending time having fun together can turn back the clock and remind you of your best moments together.

Do results like this happen immediately? No. It's not a card trick. However, being together on a daily and weekly basis can rejuvenate and rehabilitate relationships. Nurture what matters most to you, and it will grow.

....

Commit with your loved one that you will take the time to enjoy your scheduled Oases together, regardless of how you feel about each other in the moment.

"We can't agree on what to do."

Maybe you sat down with a family member and tried to discuss options by brainstorming, but you couldn't come up with something that works for both of you.

Remember, this is about them, not you.

Sitting down and having a tea party with My Little Pony's Twilight Sparkle and Pinkie Pie on the floor of my six-year-old's bedroom was not at the top of my list. I'm no closet brony.*

---

*Google it at your own risk.

But it's what she wanted. So, I set a time limit for myself that I could handle. For me: ten minutes. I went in with the mindset that I'm going to do whatever I can for the next ten minutes to make this fun for her. I focused on what she likes so that these little moments can be more jam-packed with enjoyment for her. After all, "Friendship is magic."

Also, consider how you can bring just a touch of your personality into this. For instance, perhaps you're a little on the competitive side? I sure am. That means that when I play games with my kids, I don't let them win. It's important for them to lose sometimes. It gives them character and drive.

Now, before you go reporting me to Child Protective Services, don't think I'm some brash disciplinarian who never wants his kids to feel happy. How do I reconcile my competitive nature with the fact that my son wants to play a game with me?

I taught my son how to play chess, but I didn't just teach him the ins and outs—like how to move the pawns, how a checkmate works, and how the game ends. I took it to the next level by imbuing the experience with my own personality.

At first, I gave him a six-piece handicap. I let him take six of my pieces off the board, including the queen. That made it challenging for me and competitive for him! Once he started kicking my behind, we lowered the handicap piece by piece.

On a side note, I later saw my son playing chess with his seven-year-old sister using the opposite approach. He started with just a king and a pawn and then added a pawn in after each win. Smart kid. Even better big brother.

If you find yourself spending time with a family member and you're not engaged in the activity, shift your focus away from your boredom or frustration with the situation. Instead, ask yourself, "How can I adapt to what he or she is doing, just a tiny bit, to make it a little bit more fun for me?" Don't be afraid to get creative!

In this way, you can make an Oasis mutually enjoyable. Find a way to focus on what's enjoyable for your family member. You have your consistent Oasis scheduled. This is their time.

Protect yourself against disagreement by planning and enjoying your Personal Oases. Then enter the Family Oasis planning process with the mindset that *their* desires take priority over yours. During the Family Oasis, look for ways to reframe the activity in a way that's enjoyable to you.

With a firewall firmly established around your Family Oases, we're ready to move on to the final stage: enjoyment.

CHAPTER 14

Stage Five:
Enjoying Family Oases

Just as we did when we learned about acknowledging our Personal Oasis, let's acknowledge the Oases we share with loved ones. While dopamine helps us increase our desire to succeed every time we experience it, oxytocin and a variety of other chemicals have a role in creating a bond between us and others.

Oxytocin is sometimes referred to as the "cuddle hormone." It facilitates bonding between people, such as a parent to a child or a spouse to a spouse. For most people, it doesn't take hours of hugging or even person-to-person interaction to generate a feeling of closeness. A study by Grewen, Anderson, Girdler, and Light, published in *Behavioral Medicine*, found that brief contact with a supportive partner reduces the stress associated with difficult tasks and may even have cardiovascular benefits.

Just a little time, attention, and effort. Slow down. Take it in.

By making time to absorb and enjoy fun moments with others, we are not only improving performance but also creating a stronger neurological bond with those we care about most. As I discussed previously, when we have that stronger bond, it improves our quality of life as well as our performance at work.

But if we're moving too fast and are too absorbed in "getting things done," we forget how to enjoy spending time with loved ones. We all too often *fail to feel*.

Ella's Card

This is something that I am still working on to this day—on slowing down and taking in these moments with loved ones. What follows is a personal example. As you read it, think of the last time someone you cared about did some little, nice thing for you.

My seven-year-old daughter is the card-giver in our house. Here is the beauty she whipped up for me in a flurry of creativity:

One Friday morning, I was processing my physical inbox, just as I teach people to do in my time-management courses on LinkedIn Learning. By "processing," I refer to the act of deciding what you're going to do with an object or piece of information, when you're going to do it, and where the item belongs.

I was dutifully going through the contents of the box, asking "What, when, where? What, when, where? What, when, where?" with each item.

Then, I happened upon this card from my daughter.

Dispassionately, I asked myself, "What's the next step?"

I thought, robotically, "I'm going to file this away."

"When am I going to do it?"

Answer? "I'm going to do it now."

"Where does it belong?"

Response: Ella's folder.

So I reached for the file that I have reserved for all the wonderful little cards that she makes for me and was quickly slipping it into the manila folder.

Then, thankfully, I stopped.

I realized that here was a great moment that I had failed to feel. I was missing out on something precious. So I decided to practice what I preach and take a moment to craft a meaningful reply.

I revised my answer to "What is the next step?" to, "Give her a card in return."

I'll be honest. Artsy-craftsy I am not. Picking out stationery, finding complementary colors, and drawing cute little figures with happy little faces has never been my forte. So I got creative.

"Is there an app for this?" I wondered.

I did a search and found a website called GreetingsIsland

.com. Before long, this decora-phobic daddy was choosing from a variety of fonts, pictures, and card templates. I felt like Martha Stewart meticulously selecting which eggshell white went best with the Parisian taupe and whether or not to italicize the Mardian typeface.

The result? Well . . .

I then placed it in front of her door.

There are a few moments when you and I just get it *right*, when we get one thousand family points and earn an achievement for extra valor. This little act, which took about five extra minutes, completely made my little girl's week.

This simple example goes a step deeper, though. While she found a little extra joy, it also moved me, helping me feel a greater desire to succeed and a closeness with her that I hadn't felt before. And every time I think about or retell this story, I get a positive little pick-me-up.

A big reason why that happened is because I also used those three steps we discussed about enjoying your Personal Oasis:

Mind.
Heart.
Mouth.

You can do the same. Let's walk through the steps you'll want to take when having fun with family.

Step One: Mentally Acknowledge the Good Moments

In this case, I told myself, "That was so nice to get that card from Ella" as a reminder of how great it is spending time with her.

I do that when my daughter Darci hugs me. I tell myself, "This is great to have this hug; it's wonderful to have her give me unconditional love."

I have a coaching client who's a go-go-go, type A successful CEO. She said that this trick of slowing herself down when spending time with family—to just make a mental acknowledgment—has greatly improved her relationships. It reminds her that she can temporarily step off the treadmill of success when spending time with loved ones.

Step Two: Emotionally Acknowledge It by Asking Yourself, "How Did That Make You Feel?"

With Ella, I thought, "I'm having fun creating this card for her right now. I'm surprised that doing this is so much fun." I truly was surprised!

Perhaps you will be, too.

Your response may be as simple as, "Tonight I went on a date with my husband. I felt closer to him. It warmed my heart to spend this time with him." Don't worry, Shakespeare, you don't have to declare your love in iambic pentameter. Just take a moment to consider how you feel emotionally.

Step Three: Verbally (or in Writing) Acknowledge It

 This step is slightly different when it comes to having fun with family. For Personal Oases, you were saying it to yourself. For Family Oases, you want to say it to *them*.

Tell the person you love what it meant to spend time with them. For instance: "That card you gave me made my day." Or, "I had a blast hanging out with you today."

Maybe verbalizing isn't your thing? That's okay! Do what I did! Give them a card or a written note.

Even something small, like a hug or a kiss, can mean a lot. Heck, a side hug or punching your buddy in the arm will do! Everybody's got their own "love language," or so I've heard.

However, don't be shy about saying it out loud. It may sound goofy in your head, but simply making an effort demonstrates a lot to the other person.

Any time you follow the steps of *head*, *heart*, and *mouth*, you're strengthening the moment in your mind. You'll strengthen your personal desire to experience occasions like this with loved ones more often. It also strengthens your relationships because now this family member associates you with positive memories. You'll be building oxytocin levels in their brains, too!

Before we conclude this section, think of a positive moment that happened between you and a family member recently. Take a moment to acknowledge it mentally, emotionally, and verbally.

• •

Write down one enjoyable moment that happened between you and another person in the last day or week.

_____

_____

_____

_____

Brain. Acknowledge it mentally by thinking, "That was a great moment."

Heart. Emotionally assess how it felt by asking, "How did that make me feel?"

Mouth. Finally, let that person know how it felt. Say it, write a note, or give a hug. Do something to express that you enjoyed that moment.

Wrapping Up the Family Oasis

With just a little effort, some planning, and a smallish budget, you can enjoy Oases with your family. These meaningful breaks can have huge benefits for you and the people in your life. Your career can improve, your personal connection to these individuals can increase, and your joy in life can expand. Who doesn't want those things?

With the Personal and Family Oases both established, the Oasis equation is balanced.

You're free to stop here if you prefer, but I'm not done yet. Let's move on to how we can make the Culture of WIN a reality in any workplace.

Part Four

The Work Oasis

CHAPTER 15

Mixing Fun and Business

Are you unhappy with your job? Do you feel like your manager doesn't respect you? Do you feel like the CEO has no clue about what's going on at your level in the company? If so, you're not alone.

So many workers imagine the "perfect" work environment and strictly affix their notion of happiness to that ideal. They make the pinnacle of happiness and well-being contingent upon how well their current job lines up with the model that they've created in their mind.

A recent Gallup survey found that only about one-third of US employees consider themselves engaged at work. This means that about two-thirds could care less—or are even hostile—about the work they're doing and the company they're working for. It's even worse outside the United States, with over 80 percent of employees in the disengaged category. Yet companies with highly engaged workforces outperform competitors by 147 percent.

Each year, *Fortune* magazine enlists the aid of the Great Place to Work Institute to compile the *Fortune* 100 Best Companies to Work For® list. Companies covet and seek membership in this rare group. Talk about a recruiting boost! For all employees who work for the companies on the list, the phrase "this is a fun place to work" most highly correlated among all survey statements with this phrase: "Taking everything into account, I consider this a great place to work."

Translation: if you want a workplace that attracts and retains top talent, make it a fun place to work. And if you want to love your work, find a way to infuse moments of fun into your day.

It's Not about Satisfaction

In a long list of the wonderful aspects of your job, odds are there's at least one annoying sliver in your pinkie finger that's making you rethink your career choices. As an employee, you ride a roller coaster of emotions fueled by the Culture of WISH. It says, "Someday, hopefully, the perfect workday will land on your lap and nuzzle you like a kitten. In the meantime, buck up! Just put your head down and plow ahead. That's how your forefathers' forefathers built this land, after all."

By sacrificing immediate fun in the hopes of getting some joy down the line, you're falling victim to fallacy. Here's a little secret that you may not be aware of: everybody does stuff that they don't want to do at work.

I'm sure there are plenty of readers of this book who would say they love their job but can find something about it they despise. My nemesis? Editing. Yuck.* While we can occasionally delegate portions of job ugliness, for neither you nor me is there such a thing as the 100 percent perfect job. If we sit around waiting for the perfect job to throw us the keys and "have a good time," we're always going to feel as if we're being cheated.

However, the Culture of WIN creates a different reality. It gives us the right to predetermined breaks that we can use to step away, regardless of the experiences that we may be having at the moment. Whether we're happy or unhappy with our job is irrelevant. The point is that we can take these breaks to make sure that it is always worth it *now.* That it will be worth it each day, week, month, and year.

In this way, we can be happy at work regardless of externalities. As the Dalai Lama once said: "If you have fear of some pain or suffering, you should examine whether there is anything you can do about it. If you can, there is no need to worry about it; if you cannot do anything, then there is also no need to worry." Translation: you can do something about your happiness at work, so there's no need to worry.

Who bears responsibility for making these changes? In my experience, and with a nonscientific estimate, here is how I see the "fun responsibility" divvied up in the workplace. Enjoy this tasty pie chart on the next page:

That big fat slice says that you are mostly in control of your workplace happiness. No need to sit around waiting for someone to swoop down from the heavens and save the day.

---

*At this moment, while I'm reviewing the copious red notes the copyeditor made to my manuscript, I'm suppressing a touch of nausea.

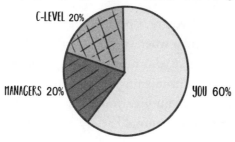

CULTURE OF WIN RESPONSIBILITY

C-LEVEL 20%

MANAGERS 20%

YOU 60%

A Different Kind of Oasis

In a workday context, it's helpful to look at meaningful breaks in terms of productivity. And in the land of meaningful breaks, the concept of ultradian rhythm is king.

The what rhythm? You've likely heard of the circadian rhythm, which is the biological flow of the day, typically applied to optimal sleep/awake cycles. The ultradian rhythm is a clever chronobiology term for a cycle that repeats many times in a day. We have a variety of ultradian rhythms, from heart rate to body-temperature regulation to appetite to even nostril dilation. You read that right.

In a workplace context, you have an optimal cycle for how long you can work until you need to take a break. Noted sleep researcher, Nathaniel Kleitman, gets credit for discovering the "basic rest-activity cycle." He first found that we have ultradian rhythms within our sleep cycle. Then he revealed that the same pattern extends into our day.

Each person has an optimal cycle for how long they can work until needing a break—or Work Oasis. Just as each person has unique nightly sleep needs,** a person's Work Oasis

---

**The National Sleep Foundation estimates that the average adult needs seven to nine hours of sleep per night. Some outliers require as little as six or as many as ten!

needs vary from around ninety minutes to two hours per ultradian cycle.

Translation: if you're a person who needs a break every ninety minutes, then when you push past the ninety-minute mark and fail to take your needed break, every minute thereafter gives you a diminishing return. However, by taking a quick Oasis break, you give your body room to reset your clock, recharge your internal battery, and return to optimal levels of performance.

Amazing, right? The key is to find your optimal workplace ultradian rhythm and then build a schedule that supports it. The fastest way to find your unique workday ultradian rhythm is through—you guessed it—experimentation!

Start with taking a ten-minute break every ninety minutes for two weeks and see how it affects your workday. Then try one-hundred-minute intervals and evaluate your performance. Continue to adjust the time period of your breaks between ninety and one hundred twenty minutes until you find your workplace ultradian rhythm.

SELF-DEFINED FUN

Which brings us back to personal responsibility. You can create a "pause that refreshes" every workday. You need not be dependent on the table scraps of time pushed into your dish that some corporate overlord approves from on high.

In fact, that's often part of the problem.

These days, companies push "fun" programs that the leader at the top of the food chain believes will be a "killer time." Despite their best intentions, executives too often provide something to their employees that will, in fact, make them—the executives—happy.

The CEO may establish a corporate golf day. But what if a third of the company workforce despises golf? See the problem? In the end, programs such as these are all about them and their definition of what an Oasis is. The real power of having fun is when employees have the freedom to choose for themselves.

If you're a C-level exec or manager, your goal will be to create an environment where everyone gets to choose their moment of refreshment. Then get the heck out of the way!

Let's suppose you want to set up a company playroom—you know, a space designated for fun activities. Great! Just do it in a way that gives people a variety of options. A little bit of this, a little bit of that—multiple choice.

After all, every person has his or her own thing. Some people are competitive dog groomers, others are training for curling in the Winter Olympics, and some even own a pygmy goat farm on the side.* You never know! Power comes from establishing a Culture of WIN that provides the leeway to find something that matches each unique personality.

In previous chapters, you learned that the Oasis break is about what you or a family member define as meaningful, fun, and refreshing. Additionally, it's ideal for employees to control when these breaks occur. Optimally, employees would create a schedule that matches their own unique productivity

---

* I've yet to see a company rec room devoted to pygmy goats. But anything is possible.

rhythm. People have certain hours of the day when they perform better than others. Mandating that everyone take a break at 10 a.m. will infringe on individuals who brag about being the Michael Jordan of 10 a.m. We want to, as best we can, avoid getting in the way of productivity.

In summary, you are in control of your own level of enjoyment. You can use the techniques that I shared earlier in the book for how to enjoy having fun. So why worry?

LESS-EFFECTIVE EXAMPLES

Before we look at companies that are properly building a Culture of WIN, let's consider a couple of less-effective approaches.

Marissa Mayer, former CEO of the now-gutted Yahoo and once a Google engineer, said that during Google's formative years, it was possible to work 130 hours per week if "you're strategic about when you sleep, when you shower, and how often you go to the bathroom."

Wow. One can argue that Google's success came about because of this mindset. I would argue that it came *despite* it. For a handful of IPO-crazed kids with a gaggle of stock options looking to be the next Google, scheduled bathroom breaks may be a wonderful motivator. For the rest of us, not so much.

The Culture of WISH is a dangerous gamble that puts too much pressure on employees. The burnout, turnover, and health implications are frightening.

Don't believe me yet?

Consider the case of Goldman Sachs, which in June 2015 encouraged employees to go home by midnight and not to come to work before 7 a.m. A policy was created prohibiting interns from working more than seventeen hours in one day.

You read that right. A *limit* of seventeen hours per day. And that was a new policy . . . for interns.

What caused the company to enact such a generous and sweeping improvement in the quality of life for its employees?* This was a breakneck, win-at-any-cost culture created by the promise of making it to the top, someday . . . hopefully. What would prompt a financial giant to draw back?

It began when, tragically, a Bank of America intern was found dead in his shower. Doctors believe the cause of death stemmed from epileptic seizures due to working seventy-two hours straight.

Yet just two years earlier, Goldman Sachs CEO Lloyd Blankfein had begun encouraging his employees to take up hobbies and take weekends off. He was quoted as saying, "You have to be interesting. You have to have interests away from the narrowing thing of what you do. You have to be somebody who somebody else wants to talk to."

Why was there such a disconnect between the words and actions of the CEO and his employees? Was it a case of a CEO saying one thing publicly while privately demanding something else from his employees? In my experience, no. Most often, it's the Culture of WISH slowly creeping its way into our offices while we tap away at our computers unaware.

Some people may argue that working overtime and losing sleep are the price of success. If you want to be the champ, you have to take the punches. You need to work long hours. You need to sacrifice. You need to be willing to put your health on the line.

Me? I say hogwash! People can achieve more if they utilize the power of a meaningful break. It is less hazardous to their

---

* I wrote that in my most sarcastic voice possible.

health physically, socially, mentally, and emotionally. It certainly is better for employee morale and retention. There is a huge cost to creating a company that is based on relentless, nonstop work. It must be avoided at every position. Not just for productivity but for profitability as well.

EFFECTIVE EXAMPLES

Let's consider some positive examples of big, successful companies that are embracing the power of having fun.

I regularly team up with LinkedIn for many courses in its Learning library. While working with its employees, I get to see firsthand the culture they've created.

LinkedIn offers monthly events called InDays—a wonderful example of how to facilitate a monthly Oasis for your company. On an InDay, LinkedIn encourages its employees to innovate, think creatively, or work on inspirational projects. It offers monthly themes for these InDays that provide a great degree of flexibility. These themes are simply guideposts to give the employees ideas of what to do with their day. This is, essentially, a monthly Oasis. Does this lead to success? LinkedIn boasts a top-ten ranking on Glassdoor as one of the best "large" places to work, and CEO Jeff Weiner holds a top-five CEO ranking.

A friend of mine works for Pixar. When the company isn't developing heartwarming stories or completely changing the way animation is made and distributed, it's creating opportunities for employees to have a bit of fun on the side. There's a massive playroom at the studio in Emeryville, California. Pixar also encourages employees to have projects outside work. These are self-designed breaks from the norm that allow them to express themselves in new ways, such as non-animation-related art projects. Imagine how external creativity contributes to the company's internal performance. In fact, you don't have to imagine because you can see the results year in and year out on the big screen, not to mention box-office returns and awards received! This policy could be compared to a monthly or even a weekly or yearly Oasis.

Kiva.org, described by *Fortune* magazine as the "hottest non-profit on the planet," is a microfinance nonprofit with a cause close to my heart. It creates a specific kind of Oasis for its employees: adult recess—essentially, a thirty-minute daily Oasis to snack, listen to music, or engage in any kind of unstructured playtime. After all, a day of alleviating poverty sure can build up your appetite!

Now it's time for us to move from just reading about these fun examples to making it happen in your workplace. In the following chapters, we're going to consider positive steps that everyone on the organization chart can take, from the top executives to managers to every single employee regardless of position.

CHAPTER 16

The Executive Level

The tippy top of the organization chart is often referred to as *C-level*, because of the *C* you find in CEO, CFO, CIO, or CAO—chief awesomeness officer—or whatever hip water-cooler acronym is currently in style. That *C* stands for *chief* because you're the head honcho. The big cheese. The alpha.

However, for our exercise, *C* is for culture, and that's good enough for me. Your perspective at the top of the organization chart is pivotal to the culture of your business.

The Power of Example

A business is the mirror of its leadership. Your personality will be reflected in the company culture, for good or for bad.

Let's suppose that, just occasionally, you allow yourself to work one hundred plus hours per week. Your employees, who begin to see that as the standard, will begin to mimic your behavior. Before long, they will be burned out and maybe even begin looking for work elsewhere. You'll be without employees. You'll go from C-level to below sea level. Time to turn this ship around!

If you are on the C-level, the most important thing is to create Personal and Family Oases for yourself, ensuring scheduled breaks daily, weekly, monthly, and yearly for yourself and your family. In doing so, you will be leading by example.

A Vision of Win

Next, when it comes to your company, let's begin—as the great guru Covey once said—with the end in mind. Pause for a moment, and consider your answer to this question:

Five years from now, what kind of company culture do you imagine? Write your answer in one or two sentences.

_____

_____

_____

_____

Do you see your people stuck in the Culture of WISH, hoping that someday all the work invested in your empire will finally pay off? Or do you see a group of people who are energized and excited each and every day because they feel their work is worth it now? What would a company filled with people with that kind of attitude become?

. . . .

Write down a few specific improvements you want to make to company culture.

_____

_____

_____

_____

Later, you can return to your sketched-out notes and create a more official company document to share with your team and help them see the vision.

. . . .

Schedule some time in your calendar to refine your company-culture vision to include having fun as a priority.

Consider the Cost

Let's address the investment you may be looking at. Most C-level execs will intuitively see the value of adopting a Culture of WIN. However, if you need a bit more justification, let me help you out.

Consider the cost associated with each employee on your payroll. Imagine that one of your best employees leaves. Either she becomes burned out or another company already living the Culture of WIN comes along and cherry picks her. What is the cost of *that* shakeup? Thousands of dollars? Tens of thousands? Hiring, firing, transition, and retraining, not to mention possible headhunter fees, can add up faster than a math professor counting cards in Vegas.

Next, consider the impact of a 2 percent increase in productivity gained by adopting a Culture of WIN. Based on field experience, I'd make a guess that the boost from taking small, meaningful breaks is closer to 5 to 15 percent. But 2 percent is a nice, safe, conservative estimate. This would yield one extra workweek of productivity from every employee, every single year. What's the ROI for *that* kind of a boost?

Finally, consider the impact of new referrals from both potential customers and employees. Your team is the greatest group of potential advocates—or detractors—your company can have. Imagine a plethora of people who continually rave about your company to others because you've made it so simple for them to enjoy their Oases. That's the kind of marketing goodwill no PR company can buy for you.

· ·

Take a moment to write your best-guess answers to the questions below.

1. What is our company's estimated cost of replacing one top-performing employee?

_____

2. What is the financial value of getting a 2 percent increase (one extra workweek per year) from every company employee?

---

3. What is the estimated marketing value of having employees who are raving fans?

Getting the picture? The investment you make in the Culture of WIN pays off and then some.

Motivating Your People

The next step is to get your merry band of misfits on board. They'll need a smidge of motivation. You could share that vision you created earlier. Discussing the financial benefits with them is another good start. You may want to hold a formal meeting to discuss principles from *The Power of Having Fun* and explore ways to begin adopting Oases into your company culture.

Nothing is more motivational, however, than giving your employees the opportunity to find their own ways to have fun. You could create your own presentation. You could share this book. You could bring me in to speak.* The choice is yours.

The key here is to make it a company-wide initiative—not just something trickled down via managers. The more your people see your commitment and passion for this cultural shift, the more excited they will be to make it a part of their day.

---

*Visit **DaveCrenshaw.com** if you're interested.

Schedule a meeting with your leadership team to discuss the following questions:

- What might we do, multiple times a day, to facilitate our employees taking meaningful, self-planned breaks? (Think of these occurring every ninety minutes or so, and lasting about ten to twenty minutes.)
- What might we do on a weekly basis? (Think of these lasting one to three hours.)
- What might we do on a monthly basis? (Think of these lasting a half-day to one day.)
- What can we do on a yearly basis to better encourage our employees to take meaningful vacations?

The Executive Checklist

Let's wrap up this chapter on the C-level by providing you with a quick checklist. Each one is in approximate order based on the amount of investment it will take in terms of time and money.

Review the following checklist and check off any actions you've already completed. Then schedule some time to complete the first item you have not yet completed.

☐ I have clearly defined and scheduled my Personal Oases.

☐ I keep and enjoy my scheduled Personal Oases.

☐ I have clearly defined and scheduled my Family Oases.

☐ I keep and enjoy my scheduled Family Oases.

☐ I have experimented with and found my optimal work-day ultradian rhythm.

☐ I have created a written vision of how my company would look if we embraced the Culture of WIN.

☐ I have done a simple analysis of the financial benefits and costs of implementing a Culture of WIN.

☐ We have trained our employees on a company-wide level about *The Power of Having Fun.*

☐ I have brainstormed options for Work Oases with the leadership team.

☐ We have created a daily Work Oasis policy (e.g., flexible break time).

☐ We have created a weekly Work Oasis policy (e.g., half-day or weekly get-together).

☐ We have created a monthly Work Oasis policy (e.g., activity day).

☐ We have created a yearly Work Oasis policy (e.g., mandatory yearly vacation).

☐ We regularly review and update the effectiveness of our Work Oasis policies.

CHAPTER 17

The Management Level

Okay, managers. Question time! Wouldn't it be wonderful if every executive in your company read this book and agreed with it? That would be fantastic, right? Being a manager would be so much easier.

Some companies are more flexible and open when it comes to this stuff. Yet for most, the life of middle management is a realm of limited control. Painful yet true.

For the purpose of this chapter, let's assume the worst-case scenario. Let's imagine that you, as a manager, are essentially on an island when it comes to this Oasis stuff. The C-level execs haven't gotten their hands on this book yet—let alone read it and agreed with it. No employees who work under you have any idea about the Culture of WIN or Oases or any of this cool stuff. You're the only person in your company who has read this book.

What is your next move? Do you even have a move to make?

You should. Per the Kelly Global Workforce Index, 63 percent of employees claim their managers have a direct influence on their job satisfaction. Additionally, 74 percent feel less loyalty toward their employer than a year ago. If you take a moment to read between those two lines, there are a couple of hidden messages:

(a) You're directly contributing to the level of satisfaction of your employees.

(b) There's likely a lot of room for improvement.

The Culture of WIN will help you regain control. Let's look at steps you can take almost immediately.

Live It

As you might expect, you can and should establish your own Personal and Family Oases. Even if these must occur outside the flow of the normal workday, you can still establish control for yourself. Take thirty minutes for your favorite show each day. Go for a hike each week. Whatever floats your personal boat.

If you have flexibility in your day, build Work Oases around your personal ultradian rhythm. One manager I coached decided to use a boxing interval timer to establish a ninety-minute reminder to stop and have some fun. Once you find your groove, you can make it more official by scheduling the breaks into your workday.

As others around you, particularly those you lead, see the results that these meaningful breaks have on your performance and productivity, they will want to do the same. In other words, people will do as you do.

Encourage Your Team

You can encourage those you manage to create their own Oases. In the next team meeting you have, teach a principle or two from this book. If you need help, just search my blog at **DaveCrenshaw.com** for videos about *The Power of Having Fun.* You'll find some free, helpful resources that you can use for a future training session.

Be aware of the emotional and physical condition of your employees. Are they starting to slow down? Do their eyes have that glazed over, running-on-Red-Bull-alone look? Is there a new subtext of frustration or hostility in their communication because they've been pulling too many all-nighters?

If so, when and where appropriate, encourage them to take and plan meaningful breaks. The key here is not to tell them what you would do. Instead, ask them what they do when they need a pick-me-up. Something like this: "When you need a break, what do you like to do for fun to recharge your batteries?" Then, whatever their answer, encourage them to do it at their earliest convenience—then come back to work with a little boost of energy.

You know how it can get. Occasionally, office demands pile up, and everyone needs to pull together to work unusual hours for a week or two. You and I wish it didn't happen, but sometimes it does. In those stretches, there is still a lot of power in pausing and considering, "When can I next take a break?" Then schedule that time in your calendar. Encourage your team members to do the same.

Plan some time to meet with team members and share a principle or two from this book.

Is there a member of your team who is showing signs of

burnout? Consider encouraging them to take or plan a meaningful break.

Make the Case

Ever have that experience where you have this A-MAZING idea that the company should implement? That if they just listened to you, they'd make more money and work would be more productive? And then you share this fantastic idea, and it stops cold at the C-level, like a pebble smacking a brick wall? If you're making an effort to be innovative, you're likely familiar with this experience.

The reason why most people don't buy into the change is that they are understandably skeptical. Few people want to put their neck on the line for your wonderful hunch. They need evidence.

Which is why we want to remove the guesswork from the Culture of WIN. I've claimed that if your team plans meaningful breaks, productivity will improve. I've cited some studies and evidence to show that longevity, performance, and employee retention will increase if you use this system. But don't take my word—or any researcher's word—for it.

Test it!

Begin by measuring where you are right now before implementing the Culture of WIN. Most companies have some metrics or numbers they use to gauge their teams' performance. Customer complaints resolved. Sales conversions. Widgets per hour. Whatever number your company uses, start with that.

Then, ninety days after you've tried to implement the principles in this book, reassess your performance. My belief is that you'll see a dramatic increase.

If so, then you can show the results to the next layer of management. Perhaps give them a copy of this book and let them know about the experiment you've been running. See whether they're interested in creating their own Oases and running an experiment on a larger scale. Take this approach, and, in most cases, you'll find more buy-in. Why? Because you'll have moved past what some dude from Utah wrote in a book: you'll now have evidence.

People can and will come around to this way of thinking, but it must be done in the proper order. We didn't begin our exploration in this book by encouraging wholesale policy revisions that could potentially cost a company a lot of money and time. No, we first took a look at the power of taking a little break to have more fun. We started with a spoonful of sugar—not the medicine.

. . . .

Identify the numbers your company uses to measure your team's performance. Make a note of where you are currently:

_____

_____

After encouraging your team to take more Oases for ninety days, reassess your team's performance using those same numbers:

_____

_____

The Checklist

If you're a manager, here's your checklist in rough order of investment:

☐ I have clearly defined and scheduled my Personal Oases.

☐ I keep and enjoy my scheduled Personal Oases.

☐ I have clearly defined and scheduled my Family Oases.

☐ I keep and enjoy my scheduled Family Oases.

☐ I have experimented with and found my optimal work-day ultradian rhythm.

☐ I encourage team members to take a meaningful break of their own choosing when I see that they need it.

☐ I have trained my team about *The Power of Having Fun.*

☐ We have identified the key numbers our company uses to measure team performance and have a record of our current level of performance.

☐ We have implemented the Oasis system among our team members and have tracked the progress of our performance after ninety days.

☐ I have shared concepts from *The Power of Having Fun* with my manager.

☐ I have presented the results of our ninety-day Oasis experiment to my managers or C-level executives.

CHAPTER 18

The Employee Level

As the song goes, "One is the loneliest number." Sometimes you're flying solo, a lone wolf. Whether you are in a company of ten or a company of tens of thousands, sometimes you just can't get managers, C-level executives, or anyone else on board. Maybe you're the only person who bought *The Power of Having Fun*, let alone the only person who bought into the message.

Remember, you are in control. Even if both your management and C-level executives combined were against this policy 100 percent, you could still have fun and be refreshed. Even if you're flipping burgers and dunking fries at minimum wage, you still control your destiny. Like He-Man and the Masters of the Universe, you have the power.*

Let's take a look at what you can do with all that power.

---

*Bonus points if you mightily lift this book over your head and shout at the top of your lungs, "By the power of Crenshaw, I have the POWER!"

Own Your Oasis

First, creating your Oases outside work hours is always in play. Always.

Worst-case scenario: You're working two jobs with little time to spare. You could still create a daily Personal Oasis of just five minutes to sit still, take some deep breaths, and listen to that favorite song of yours at full blast. That's your Oasis, and no one can take it from you. Don't let them. Your long-term livelihood depends upon it.

It's critical to not fool yourself into thinking that you'll take your break when you have time. Wrong. Plan your Oases in advance. Add them to your calendar, and then protect them ruthlessly. Remember: it's not about deserving, it's about needing.

The same rule goes for those Family Oases. Your family needs you, and they want to be with you. Enjoying a small Oasis with them will remind you of why you're doing all this hard work in the first place. It will drive you that much more to be successful in whatever you're attempting.

Share Your Oasis

Second, you can share this with your coworkers or friends. You can talk to them about how the simple act of scheduling Oases has helped you become happier at work and at home and how it's helped you accomplish more.

You might even lend this book to a coworker and say, "Hey, let's test this out together for ninety days." There's a lot of positive peer-pressure power in getting a friend to experiment along with you.

Implement both the Family and Personal Oases with your buddy, and compare notes at the end of ninety days. Did you see an increase in productivity, happiness, and well-being? In short, don't simply take my word for it. Team up and test it.

· ·

Consider whether there is a friend or coworker who could benefit from setting up Oases. When could you talk to that person about this?

_____

_____

_____

Passing It Along

There's a bonus step for you, He-Man . . . or She-Ra.

You have the power to influence your company. More than you realize. On more than one occasion, I've seen companies that have changed for the better simply because one employee had the courage to speak up and share something he learned. That little push of the domino started a chain reaction all the way to the top. Even if you don't influence the whole company, you can certainly influence your coworkers and team.

You can bring this concept and book to the attention of your manager. Perhaps you can find a video about *The Power of Having Fun* on **DaveCrenshaw.com** and pass it along. This could become the starting point for your conversation. For best results, be sure you have been living your own Personal and Family Oasis for a couple of weeks so that you have some examples to share.

Let me give you one more option, especially if you're a cautious reader. You can also reach out to me on my website **DaveCrenshaw.com**. We can keep it confidential. The note you provide will let my team know to reach out to company leadership and see whether they're interested in taking the next step of having me come speak to them.

The Checklist

If you're an employee, here's your checklist of actions you can take in rough order of increasing investment.

☐ **I have clearly defined and scheduled my Personal Oases.**

☐ **I keep and enjoy my scheduled Personal Oases.**

☐ **I have clearly defined and scheduled my Family Oases.**

☐ **I keep and enjoy my scheduled Family Oases.**

☐ **I have experimented with and found my optimal workday ultradian rhythm.**

☐ **I have shared this book or concepts from it with a team member or friend.**

☐ **A team member and I began a ninety-day experiment testing our performance and job satisfaction.**

☐ **I have shared this book or concepts from it with a manager.**

CHAPTER 19

Having Fun Every Day

We began this book by talking about the journey through the desert. Now we've reached the end of this book's journey. If you've been putting the principles I've shared into practice, odds are you've begun to experience greater control and productivity, all while having more fun.

At this point, it's helpful to do a comparative assessment. Remember the Fun Scorecard you filled out in chapter 3? Time to take it again and compare your results.

You've got two options for retaking the quiz:

Flip back to chapter 3 and take the assessment again. Tally up your scores and compare your outcome with the first time you took the test. In which areas did you improve most?

or

Take it online at PowerofHavingFun.com/quiz. This easy-to-use version does all the heavy lifting for you. It will tabulate your responses and email you the results.

I hope you've seen improved balance in your day and now have Personal, Family, and Work Oases all working in harmony to provide a continually refreshing experience. No matter where you are in the process, there's always another step to take. Keep it light, be playful, and explore new ways to infuse your calendar with fun.

This concludes our experiment together . . . but not the conversation.

If you have any questions about concepts from this book, I'd love to help you find your answers. You can reach out to me at **DaveCrenshaw.com/ask**.

If you have a great story to share about implementing Oases in your personal, family, or work life, or if you've got some pictures of yourself enjoying an Oasis, please drop me a line. You can email me at **fun@DaveCrenshaw.com** or share via social media using the hashtag #PowerofHavingFun. I look forward to hearing from you.

Have fun!

Appendix

Your License to Have Fun

This book helped you give yourself permission to have more fun, right?

But what if you have a hard time believing it? What if you forget—occasionally—that having fun and enjoying Oases are essential to your long-term success?

Enter the License to Have Fun.

Complete this with your name, a picture (or drawing) of yourself in "fun mode," and your favorite quotation to remind you of the importance of having fun.

For a downloadable version of this license, visit **PowerofHavingFun.com**.

EXAMPLE:

CUT OUT:

LICENSE TO HAVE FUN

YOUR FUN PICTURE   YOUR NAME

FUN QUOTE

The POWER of HAVING FUN   DaveCrenshaw.com

BONUS FOR A FRIEND:

LICENSE TO HAVE FUN

YOUR FUN PICTURE   YOUR NAME

FUN QUOTE

The POWER of HAVING FUN   DaveCrenshaw.com

Personal Oasis
Brainstorming Worksheet

What do you like to do for fun? If this question stumps you, you're not alone! Many people have forgotten how to enjoy themselves.

By remembering what you used to enjoy doing, you may be able to rediscover how to find refreshment. Take a moment and brainstorm any ideas that come to mind as you remember what you used to do for fun. If you need additional ideas, refer to the lists of what kids and other adults find fun in chapter 6, "Stage Two: Discovering Your Fun."

For a downloadable version of this worksheet, visit **PowerofHavingFun.com**.

Age	What did you like to do for fun?	Why did you enjoy it?
10 years (Example)	*I liked playing with Legos*	*I enjoyed being able to create new things. Also playing pretend with friends and interacting between "characters."*
10 years		
15 years		
20 years		
25+ years		

Family Oasis Brainstorming Worksheet

Those around you are your greatest support team and contribute to your success at work. How will you connect with loved ones on a regular basis so that they experience Oases as well?

During a scheduled time, sit down with a family member and ask, "What, to you, would be a meaningful activity for us to do together?" To aid the brainstorming process, avoid editing or responding as they share ideas.

After brainstorming the initial list, for each item, ask, "Why is this activity meaningful to you?" and write a brief answer in the second column. For more information, review chapter 11, "Stage 2: Discovering Family Fun."

For a downloadable version of this worksheet, visit **PowerofHavingFun.com**.

What would be meaningful to them?	Why would it be meaningful?

Oasis Category Worksheet

Take the lists you created in the brainstorming exercises and transfer each activity that you would enjoy to the worksheet below. Categorize each idea according to the amount of time it would require. Then make a note about the estimated cost next to each activity. For further information, refer to chapters 6 and 11 on discovering fun.

For a downloadable version of this worksheet, visit **PowerofHavingFun.com**.

Length (Category)	Activities	Estimated cost
(Example) Under 15 minutes (daily)	*Sit on the porch in the evening and enjoy talking with each other for a bit*	*Zero*
Under 15 minutes (daily)		
15 to 90 minutes (daily or weekly)		
90 minutes to 12 hours (weekly or monthly)		
One half-day to 3 days (monthly or yearly)		
More than 3 days (yearly)		

ACKNOWLEDGMENTS

Many people had a hand in helping this book come together. Special thanks:

- To Faye Banzon, John Arce, and Aimee Borneo for being ever invaluable. Thank you for giving me the freedom and support behind the scenes to allow me to do what I do.

- To Michael Scurries for adding color to my words in all the right places.

- To Matt Wagner for always hustling, believing, and being patient.

- To Neal Maillet for the creative workout that got this book to where it is now.

- To Abu Khalid for the brilliant illustrations you see on these pages.

- To Jeevan Sivasubramaniam for the inspiration behind the artwork.

- To Jason Hewlett for being a true frientor and continual source of positive energy.

- To my coaching clients—past, present, and future—for allowing me the privilege of both serving and learning from you all.

- To Stratton, Ella, and Darci for showing me on a daily basis what having fun is truly about.

- Finally, to my wife, for putting up with it all. Maybe someday I'll write *How to Write a Book without Driving Your Spouse Crazy in the Process*. Then again, that would kind of defeat the point, wouldn't it?

Resources

Personally, I'm a bottom-line kind of guy—an entrepreneur at heart. This means that this book wasn't written in an academic style. That was by choice. A book about having fun should, after all, be *fun*!

Yet, in addition to the case studies from my personal clients, you'll notice that a lot of research went into the creation of this book. In many instances, studies and articles that weren't referenced directly still had a significant impact in shaping the philosophy of this book.

Some readers may want to dive deeper into the studies and the thoughts of great minds that influenced this book. That's why my team created a "Resources" section at **PowerofHavingFun.com**. There you'll find links to dozens of web pages, including the studies mentioned in the book.

Also on that site, you can download PDF files of the worksheets mentioned in this book.

Index

About the Author

Dave Crenshaw is a happily married father of three who lives in the shadow of Utah's Rocky Mountains. An admitted geek, he enjoys all things sci-fi and superhero and has an Xbox gamer score of over 75,000. He enjoys watching sports, dabbles in archery, and embarrasses himself at golf.

In addition to having fun, Dave has written several business books and is a keynote speaker at events around the world. He continually develops new courses for LinkedIn Learning, where his videos have received millions of views. His writing has appeared in numerous publications, including *Time* magazine, *USA Today*, *FastCompany*, and the BBC News. As an author, speaker, and online instructor, Dave has helped build tens of thousands of productive leaders worldwide.

Work with Dave Crenshaw

Learning

Dave's collection of online training, including the time-management courses mentioned in this book, are available through LinkedIn Learning.

Visit **DaveCrenshaw.com/courses** for quick access.

Coaching

Dave coaches a select handful of leaders. To apply for private coaching with Dave and to get a personalized plan to become more productive, take the free online assessment at **DaveCrenshaw.com/quiz**.

Speaking

Dave is available for live keynote speeches, seminars, webinars, and work-shops. You can request more information at **DaveCrenshaw.com/speak**.

Berrett–Koehler
Publishers

Berrett-Koehler is an independent publisher dedicated to an ambitious mission: *Connecting people and ideas to create a world that works for all.*

We believe that the solutions to the world's problems will come from all of us, working at all levels: in our organizations, in our society, and in our own lives. Our BK Business books help people make their organizations more humane, democratic, diverse, and effective (we don't think there's any contradiction there). Our BK Currents books offer pathways to creating a more just, equitable, and sustainable society. Our BK Life books help people create positive change in their lives and align their personal practices with their aspirations for a better world.

All of our books are designed to bring people seeking positive change together around the ideas that empower them to see and shape the world in a new way.

And we strive to practice what we preach. At the core of our approach is Stewardship, a deep sense of responsibility to administer the company for the benefit of all of our stakeholder groups including authors, customers, employees, investors, service providers, and the communities and environment around us. Everything we do is built around this and our other key values of quality, partnership, inclusion, and sustainability.

This is why we are both a B-Corporation and a California Benefit Corporation—a certification and a for-profit legal status that require us to adhere to the highest standards for corporate, social, and environmental performance.

We are grateful to our readers, authors, and other friends of the company who consider themselves to be part of the BK Community. We hope that you, too, will join us in our mission.

A BK Life Book

BK Life books help people clarify and align their values, aspirations, and actions. Whether you want to manage your time more effectively or uncover your true purpose, these books are designed to instigate infectious positive change that starts with you. Make your mark!

To find out more, visit **www.bkconnection.com**.

Berrett–Koehler
Publishers

Connecting people and ideas
to create a world that works for all

Dear Reader,

Thank you for picking up this book and joining our worldwide community of Berrett-Koehler readers. We share ideas that bring positive change into people's lives, organizations, and society.

To welcome you, we'd like to offer you a free e-book. You can pick from among twelve of our bestselling books by entering the promotional code **BKP92E** here: http://www.bkconnection.com/welcome.

When you claim your free e-book, we'll also send you a copy of our e-newsletter, the *BK Communiqué*. Although you're free to unsubscribe, there are many benefits to sticking around. In every issue of our newsletter you'll find

- A free e-book
- Tips from famous authors
- Discounts on spotlight titles
- Hilarious insider publishing news
- A chance to win a prize for answering a riddle

Best of all, our readers tell us, "Your newsletter is the only one I actually read." So claim your gift today, and please stay in touch!

Sincerely,

Charlotte Ashlock
Steward of the BK Website

Questions? Comments? Contact me at bkcommunity@bkpub.com.

MIX
Paper from
responsible sources
FSC® C002589
www.fsc.org

Certified
Corporation
bcorporation.net